THE
CHRISTIAN'S
FREEDOM.

THE CHRISTIAN'S FREEDOM

Wherein is fully expressed
the Doctrine of Christian Liberty,

by the Right Reverend Father in God,

George Downame,

Doctor of Divinity and
Lord Bishop of Derry

Soli Deo Gloria Publications
...for instruction in righteousness...

Soli Deo Gloria Publications
717 Liberty Avenue, Suite 2311
Pittsburgh, PA 15222
(412) 232-0866/FAX 232-0867

*

This edition of *The Christian's Freedom*
is taken from the Oxford edition
of 1835. This Soli Deo Gloria
reprint is 1994.

*

ISBN 1-877611-75-1

TO THE GODLY AND

CHRISTIAN READER.

GRACE, MERCY, AND PEACE.

Godliness, and Christianity are the sure Grounds of Salvation. I have here in this treatise following given thee the true Pattern of a godly life which I desire thee to peruse daily, to practise faithfully, and hold on constantly, and thou shalt be sure to have blessings in this world and everlasting happiness in the Kingdom of Heaven. When thou hast attained to live well and feel the comfort of godliness in thy heart, then be sure to set down thy resolution never to fall into the snare of ungodliness any more.

Be sure not to faint in well-doing, because the reward is not promised [a] to him that doth

a 1 Thes. vi.

but to him that continueth to do. *A threefold blessing of God, upon those which seek him he promiseth* he will awake unto them, *and for those which pray unto him,* He will make the righteousness of their habitation prosperous. *And to those which are pure and upright,* He will make their latter end increase exceedingly: *Yea though their beginning be but small.*

But defer not, put not off thy amendment from time to time least thou art sorry for thy mispent lewd life, when thou shalt not have time to repent. Therefore know, O man, whatsoever thou art, that Godliness will crown thee with honour and glory, and furnish thee with true godliness and perfect felicity, and exalt thee unto the Heavens and co-unite thee and thy soul with God.

The many excellent [b] *treatises and larger discourses concerning the power of Godliness, which it hath pleased the Lord of Glory to furnish his Church withal in these last days; as they have made good the faithfulness of our God unto us of this Church of England, so if they shall not be a witness against us, they do necessarily require the right use thereof, that we be trans-*

b Dr. Preston, Greenham, Perkins, Rogers, Bolton.

formed into the same image from glory to glory. And therefore howsoever it may seem both needless and prejudicial after so many grave, and experimental rules concerning sanctification, to add any more in this kind: yet seeing it hath pleased God to direct me to a further labour herein, weigh with me I pray thee in equity these reasons thereof.

1. *I do hereby profess my thankfulness unto God for those excellent labours of his Saints that now rest from their labours and their fruits follow them.*

2. *I would have thee know that I am not ashamed of this foolishness of preaching and practical Divinity, which is such a mystery to the world, and stumbling block unto the wisdom thereof.*

3. *Howsoever I do profess that I am not able to attain such perfection, as I have herein conceived, yet I would have thee know farther, that I would rather have a rule to condemn sin in the flesh, and so confound the old man, that thereby the new man may follow hard after the mark, than not to give testimony to that light which hath shined so graciously unto me, or to conceal my judgment, though it may condemn the practice.*

4. *May it please thee to consider with me: Can a man walk in the Sun, and not be warm, and where two lie together, will there not be heat? and can the light be hidden, nay, onght it to be hidden?*

5. *Can we do less in these days than convince a profane world?*

6. *Can we do better than strengthen that which is ready to die?*

7. *Shall not God's remembrancers renew their strength, when the Devil's instruments do so rage with all licentiousness?*

8. *Do we not justify the good by seeking out their ways?*

9. *Should we not discourage the wicked by making a good profession?*

10. *Owe we not duty to our Mother?*

11. *Shall not this redound to the Glory of God. Let this content thee: and provoke thee to make use of these labours, and the Lord give thee understanding in all things: that thou mayest try the Spirits, and hereby thine own, whether thou art in the faith or no, and so for ever mayest follow the true Shepherd. Now unto him that is able to keep you from falling, and to preserve you faultless before the presence of his glory with exceeding joy, I heartily*

*commend you, desiring that this weak labour may be carefully read, and diligently practised, that so your souls may be eternally saved in that great and dreadful day of his visitation.**

* NOTE BY THE EDITOR.

VERY scanty materials are left us from which we can derive any satisfactory information respecting the pious and learned author of the following ingenious treatise. It would appear from "Sir James Ware's Commentary of the Prelates of Ireland," that he was born in the county of Chester, but in what year is left entirely to conjecture. He was educated at the University of Cambridge, and was elected a Fellow of Christ College in the year of our Lord 1585; so that we may with good probability place his birth between A.D. 1560—1565. He was afterwards, for some time, Professor of Logic in the same University, and seems to have given much attention to this subject, of which his works in general bear ample marks. He wrote a commentary on *Ramus*, which is mentioned with high approbation by Fuller, who says that no man of that day was better skilled in this branch of learning. How long he retained his professorship does not appear; but the next event of his life of which we have any correct information is, his being appointed chaplain to King James the First, probably very soon after that Monarch succeeded to the English throne in A.D. 1603. In the year 1616 he was advanced by King James to the See of Derry. He appears to have found his diocese in a very low state of discipline, "abounding," as he says, "with all manner of delinquents, who refused obedience to all spiritual processes." We may consider it as a mark of confidence reposed in him by the government of that day, that he obtained a commission, with very extensive powers, for the suppression of these disorders in a summary manner. He appears to have resided very constantly in his diocese, and to have devoted himself very sedulously to his episcopal duties. He presided over the See of Derry for about eighteen years, and died at Londonderry A.D. 1634, about the age of 71—6.

Bishop George Downeham is carefully to be distinguished from his elder brother Dr. John Downeham, who, although far inferior to his brother as a divine, is better known as an author, probably from his writings being much more voluminous, and also of a more popular character. Both are remarkable for the very earnest strain of piety which pervades their works; but the bishop is far the superior in talent, and soundness of judgment, and accuracy, and all which can give a title to the character of a *learned Divine.*

The principal works of Bishop Downeham are :—1. On Justification. 2. On Prayer. 3. On the Lord's Prayer. 4. On the Decalogue. 5. A Defence of Episcopacy, and, 6. The following Treatise on Christian Liberty. Besides these, he wrote a Book on the Perseverance of the Saints, which was suppressed by royal proclamation, addressed to Archbishop Usher, bearing date Aug. 24, 1631. Many copies, however, of Downeham's treatise had been circulated before the order was duly published. This work is exceedingly scarce; and the Editor being unable to procure a copy, can furnish no reason for the attempt made to suppress it.

THE DOCTRINE

OF

CHRISTIAN LIBERTY.

JOHN viii. 36.

"*If therefore the Son shall make you free, you shall be free indeed.*"

Sect. 1. *The context.* THESE words are a conclusion of the verses going before. For, whereas our Saviour Christ having promised some of the hearers, who,[a] while he was yet speaking of his person and office, began to believe in him, that if they did approve themselves to be his[b] true disciples, by their perseverance and constant abiding in his word, they[c] "should know the truth," (that is, he would more fully manifest himself unto them, as he speaketh, John

a Ver. 30. b Ver. 31. c Ver. 32.

xiv. 21,) and this "truth, (which is himself, John xiv. 6,[d]) should make them free;" the captious Jews (pretending that they understood him as speaking of a corporeal or civil liberty)[e] cavilled at this promise, which indeed did not belong unto them, as if he had offered them great indignity, by promising them liberty, to presuppose their servitude; alledging that they were already free, and therefore scorned his promised liberty, which they needed not, being neither servants by nature or birth, for they *were Abraham's seed,* nor yet by their fortune or personal condition, for they *never served any.* Our Saviour, therefore, both to refute their cavil, and also to justify his promise, proveth these four things unto them: 1. That they were servants. 2. That they had great need to be made free. 3. That this freedom must come by him. 4. That being freed by him, they should be free indeed.

The first he proveth thus:[f] "whosoever committeth sin," that is, in whomsoever sin reigneth, *he is the servant of sin;* but such he insinuateth they were, yea, such are all men[g] by nature, until they be ingrafted into Christ by faith, and renewed by the Holy Ghost; and therefore he would have them to conclude, that for all their brags, they

d John xiv. 6. 21.
e Ver. 33.
f Ver. 34.
g Tit. iii. 3.

were the miserable servants of sin, and consequently the slaves of Satan,[h] subject to the curse of the law, and to eternal damnation.

(2.) That they had great need to be made free, he showeth both by the inconvenience of their servitude; for being[i] servants,[k] and not sons, howsoever now they had a place in the house of God, as Ishmael[l] had; yet the time should come, that they should be cast out;) and also by the benefit which should accompany their freedom, that being made the *sons* of God, they should as heirs of eternal life, *abide*, not only to the end of their days, in the church militant,[m] (which is the house of God upon earth,) but also for ever in the church triumphant, which is God's[n] house in heaven.

(3.) That the faithful attain to this freedom by adoption in Christ. For, to "so[o] many as receive him by faith, he hath given this liberty or power to be the sons of God." And,[p] "if sons, then also heirs." This assertion is presupposed in this place, as being the hypothesis whereupon this inference is grounded. Those that be the sons of God, abide in the house of God for ever; therefore, if the son shall make you

h 1 John iii. 8. i Ver. 35. k Slaves.
l Gen. xxi. 10. m Tim. iii. 15. n John xiv. 1.
o John i. 12; Gal. iii. 26.
p Rom. viii. 17; Gal. iv. 7.

free, &c., presupposing that men attain to the freedom of God's sons, by the benefit of Christ, the only begotten Son of God.

Whereupon, as I said, is referred the fourth thing, which is my text; "If the Son therefore shall make you free, you shall be free indeed."

As if he had said: you have no cause to cavil at the promise of liberty, which I make to all them which truly believe in me. For I tell you upon my word, which is amen, (that is, true and infallible,) that both you, and all men by nature, though the seed of Abraham (as you are), though living (as you do) in the visible church of God, are the very servants of sin; that being servants and not sons, they must not look to inherit[q] with the sons of the promise, or to abide in the house for ever; but when the time of separation cometh, they shall as[r] chaff, be severed from the wheat; as tares, from the corn; as goats, from the sheep; as[s] Hagar and Ishmael, from Isaac the son of the promise. Therefore, though your pride will not suffer you to see and acknowledge thus much; yet certainly great need have you to be made free; that of the servants of sin, you may become the sons of God. But

q Gal. iv. 28. r Matt. iii. 12, 13; xxx. 25, 33.
s Gen. xxi. 10; Gal. iv. 30.

you, who are (as all[t] men by nature are) the children of wrath, cannot possibly be the sons of God, except you believe in me, who am the only begotten Son of God; that I may by the grace of adoption communicate that unto you, which I myself am by nature and eternal generation. So shall you, of the servants of sin, sons of Satan, and heirs of hell and damnation, be made the sons of God, heirs of eternal life, citizens and free denizens of the kingdom of heaven. Whereas, now therefore you are miserable servants, notwithstanding your corporeal and carnal liberty, whereof you vaunt, which is not a true liberty, but a voluntary service of sin: if you shall believe in me, and approve yourselves to be my true disciples, by abiding in my words; I, who am the truth, will make you free, not with a counterfeit or imaginary freedom, such as is your liberty, but with a true and spiritual freedom, which is the gracious, and the glorious liberty of the sons of God.

Thus have you heard the context, or coherence of these words with the former, (whereunto we are referred by this word of inference, *therefore*) wherein divers things might profitably be observed, but that the text calleth me unto it, as containing matter of greatest importance.

t Ephes. ii. 3.

Sect. 2. The text. The argument whereof is Christian liberty.

For Christian liberty, which is the argument of my text, is, as the Apostle saith,[a] τὸ ἀγαθὸν ἡμῶν the very good of Christians; which Christ our Saviour, taking upon him the form of a servant, hath purchased with his own most precious [b] blood, which is the benefit of the Messiah, whereunto we are called,[c] Gal. v. 13, which he hath promised as a reward to his true disciples,[d] ver. 32, which as himself came to preach,[e] Luke iv. 18, so doth he send us, his ambassadors to the same end, viz. to preach the Gospel, which is the [f] *law of liberty*, and the doctrine of redemption and freedom by him; that by our Ministry[g] men may be brought out of spiritual bondage, unto the liberty of God's children. The consideration whereof, as it bindeth me with all reverent care and intention of mind, to entreat of this argument; so ought it to move you to hear the same with great diligence and attention. And the rather, not only because among us, who profess the Gospel, many do not know the Christian liberty, and more do abuse it to their own perdition; but also because the Papists are both enemies of the liberty itself, endeavouring by their Antichristian doctrine,

a Rom. xiv. 16. b 1 Peter i. 18. c Gal. v. 13.
d John viii. 32. e Luke iv. 18. f James i. 25; ii. 12.
g Acts xxvi. 18.

to bereave us of the chief parts thereof, and also malicious slanderers of the most Christian and comfortable doctrine of our churches concerning the same.

The explication of the text. But to come to the words of my text, the sum and effect whereof is this: that "Christ the Son of God, is the author of true liberty, to all those that truly believe in him." For the explication whereof, we are first to speak of this liberty in general, and afterwards to descend unto the particulars. In the general doctrine we are to consider these four things. 1. What it is, and wherein generally it doth consist. 2. Who is the author of this liberty, which in the text is expressed to be the only begotten Son of God. 3. The subject, or the parties on whom this liberty is conferred, which is plainly gathered out of the context, or inference of these words upon the former, to be all the sons of God by adoption. 4. The general property of this liberty, that it is not a counterfeit or imaginary, but a true liberty. Of all which points, I will speak very briefly.

The general doctrine of Christian liberty.

Sect. 3. The definition of Christian liberty. As touching the first: for as much as logicians teach,[a] that the definition of the special, is to be fetched from the distribu-

a Arist. Poster. i. 14.

tion of the general; for which cause, the[b] Divine Philosopher calleth a distribution *βασίλικον λόγον*, as being the ready, and as ït were the King's way to a definition: we will therefore take a survey of the divers sorts of liberty. For there is an outward and external liberty, and there is an inward or internal liberty. The former is the liberty of the outward man from external or bodily servitude, which may be called the corporeal or civil liberty. Of this our Saviour speaketh not, though the Jews would seem so to understand him; but of the internal, which may well stand with the outward or civil bondage. For as our Saviour Christ noted them,[c] though outwardly free, to be in spiritual bondage: so contrariwise, those who in respect of the inner man are free, may notwithstanding be subject to the external or civil servitude; which nothing impeacheth or impaireth the liberty of the soul and conscience before God. In which regard the Apostle saith, "[d] He that is called in the Lord, being a servant, is the Lord's freeman." So that the liberty whereof we speak, is a liberty of the soul, or inner man. Wicked therefore is the doctrine of the Anabaptists, who thereby exempt themselves from all subjection to the civil magistrate, under pretence of Christian liberty. I call their doctrine wicked, be-

b Plato in Sophista. c John viii. 33, 34.
d 1 Cor. vii. 21.

cause the Apostle Peter[e] saith, that they who under pretence of Christian liberty deny obedience to the magistrate in lawful things, do use their liberty for a cloak to cover their wickedness.

Again, the inward liberty is either a carnal or spiritual liberty. The carnal liberty is that whereby the soul of man is free from righteousness; which indeed is a voluntary service of sin. For when men be free from righteousness, they are servants of sin, and contrariwise, as the Apostle[f] sheweth. But our Saviour speaketh of a liberty, which, as it freeth men from servitude and sin, and all the spiritual yokes of bondage, which accompany the same; so it maketh them the servants of righteousness. For when "we are[g] made free from sin, we are made the servants of righteousness." Wherefore, as in respect of the former, we say with the Apostle, He that is called, being a servant, is the freeman of Christ: so in respect of this latter, [h] he "that is called being free, is the servant of Christ." Devilish therefore is the doctrine of the Libertines, who under pretence of Christian liberty, discharge Christians from all obedience to the law of God, setting them free to do whatsoever themselves think good. And such is the slander of the

e 1 Pet. ii. 16. f Rom. vi. 20.
g Rom. vi. 18. h 1 Cor. vii. 22.

Papists, laying that doctrine to our charge, who notwithstanding are further from it than themselves. For, by the Pope's indulgences and pardons and the Priest's absolutions, setting men free from sin for small and oft-times for ridiculous penances, what do they else but teach men to make but a sport of sin? Of such libertines the Apostle Peter [i] speaketh, that whilst they promise liberty to others, themselves are the servants of corruption.

It remaineth therefore, that Christian liberty is a spiritual liberty, freeing the true Christian from the servitude of sin, and from all other yokes of spiritual bondage, wherewith sin had entangled us.

Neither is Christian liberty only privative, as being a freedom and immunity from bondage; as though this were all, that by it we are not servants; but as appeareth by this Scripture, it is also positive, as being a liberty, power, right, and interest to the privileges of God's children, who are also heirs of God and coheirs with Christ. For when he had said that servants abide not in the house for ever, but that such as be sons, abide in the house of God for ever, he inferreth, If therefore the Son shall make you free, you shall be free indeed. Giving us to understand, that those whom he freeth, he doth

i 2 Pet. ii. 19.

not only make them not servants, viz. of sin, but also sons and heirs of God and citizens of heaven. Even as they who are made freemen of London, or any other terrestial city, are not only exempted from being servants or apprentices, but also are endowed with the liberties and privileges of free burgesses and citizens. So saith the Apostle [k], Gal. iv. 5. that Christ hath redeemed those who were under the law, that we might receive the adoption of sons, &c.

Christian liberty therefore is a spiritual liberty, which as the [l] Apostle speaketh, the faithful have in Christ Jesus. That is the definition.

The partition. The essential parts whereof generally it consisteth, are two. For partly it is privative, as being an immunity from all spiritual bondage; in which respect it is called in the Scripture [m] λύτρωσις and [n] ἀπολύτρωσις, that is redemption, and is sometimes expressed by the verbs [o] ἀπαλλάττεσθαι and [p] ρύεσθαι, signifying deliverance: and partly it is positive, as being a right, title, and interest to the privileges and prerogatives of God's adopted children in Christ, the citizens of the celestial Jeru-

k Gal. iv. 5, 6, 7. l Galat. ii. 4. ἐλευθερία ἡμῶν ἣν ἔχομεν ἐν Χριστῷ Ἰησοῦ. m Heb. ix. 12. Luke ii. 38. n Rom. iii. 24. Colos. i. 14. o Heb. ii. 15. p Colos. i. 13. 1 Thess. i. 10.

2. The AUTHOR of Christian Liberty — Jesus — the Son.
Listed below are a host of scriptures, which speak of the completeness of this work

salem: and it is called ἐξουσία, as John i. 12, those that receive Christ by faith, he hath given ἐξουσιαν, liberty, right or power to be the sons of God, 1 Cor. viii. 9. Take heed, lest [q] ἡ ἐξουσία ὑμῶν your liberty, right, or power, be not an offence to the weak. Thus you see what this liberty is, and wherein generally it doth consist.

Sect. 4. The efficient or author of this liberty.

The author of this liberty is Christ the Son of God, as it is here said; "If the Son therefore shall make you free," &c. so the Apostle calleth it [a] "the liberty which we have in and by Christ:" and again, [b] the "liberty wherewith Christ hath made us free." For he is ὁ ῥυόμενος [c] that "Deliverer which should come out of Zion," who "delivereth us[d] from the wrath of God," from the tyranny of Satan,[e] dissolving the works of the devil,[f] binding the strong man and casting him out,[g] spoiling principalities and powers, and [h] leading captivity captive; from the bondage of sin, for he is the [i] "Lamb of God that taketh away the sins of the world," whose blood doth [k] cleanse us both from the guilt of sin, and also from the corruption: for therefore "he

q 1 Cor. viii. 9. a Galat. ii. 4. b Galat. v. 1.
c Rom. xi. 26. d 1 Thess. i. 10. e 1 John iii 8.
f Matt. xii. 29. g Colos. ii. 15. h Ephes. iv. 8.
i John i. 7. k John i. 7; Heb. ix. 14; 1 Peter i. 18.

[l] gave himself for us, that he might redeem us from all iniquity, and might purge us to be a peculiar people to himself, zealous of good works." And he is that perfect Saviour, out of whose side did issue both [m] "blood and water;" the blood of redemption, to free us from the guilt of sin; and the water of ablution, to cleanse us from the corruption. From the law, [n] for "therefore was he born of a woman, and made under the law, that he might redeem them that were under the law." From death and damnation; for therefore he became a [o] "curse," that we might be freed from the curse; therefore he died, that "through [p] death he might vanquish him, who had the power of death, that is, the devil; and that he might deliver them, who through fear of death, were all their life time subject to bondage."

But this needeth no proof; for in that we profess him to be our redeemer, by whom we have [q] redemption, we all acknowledge him to be the author of our liberty. Let us rather consider, how he procureth this liberty unto us. This he doth two ways; both meritoriously, and effectually. By his merit, in [r] "giving himself to be a price of ransom for us." For, as Peter [s] saith, we "are redeemed

l Tit. ii. 14. m John xix 34, 35; 1 John v. 6.
n Gal. iv. 4. o Gal. iii. 13. p Heb. ii. 14, 15.
q Ephes. i. 7; 1 Cor. i. 30. r 1 Tim. ii. 6.
s 1 Pet. i. 18, 19.

not with any corruptible things, as silver and gold, but with the precious blood of Christ," by [t] which "blood he is entered once into the holy place, having procured an eternal redemption for us." Secondly, by the efficacy of his spirit, for we are not to imagine, that Christ hath only merited and purchased this liberty for us; but that also he doth confer, apply, and bestow it upon us: which he doth by giving unto us his "[u] Spirit." For, as in the natural body, the animal spirit, which causeth sense and motion, is from the head sent into all the members of the body; so in the mystical body of Christ, the "Spirit of [x] liberty" is communicated to all his members; by which spirit he dwelleth in us, and effectually worketh this liberty, in the degrees of our salvation, viz. vocation, justification, sanctification, glorification, (as you shall hear anon,) and by the means of our salvation. The principal whereof is the preaching of the Gospel, which is the "Law," [y] or doctrine of liberty, the ministry whereof was ordained to this end, to "[z] open men's eyes, to turn them from darkness unto light, and from the power of Satan unto God, that by faith in Christ, they may receive forgiveness of sins, and inheritance with them that be sanctified."

t Heb. ix. 12. u Rom. viii 9, 19.; Gal. iv. 6.
x Psalm. li. 14. y James i. 25. z Acts xxvi. 18.

How should we LIVE in response to our Christian Liberty? Note the points below – especially point (5), which emphasizes our VALUE of the freedom which cost Jesus everything – and the NEED to acknowledge that I am NOT my own!

The use of this doctrine concerning the author of our liberty.

This teacheth us, (1) that in ourselves we are servants, (for else we needed not a redeemer) and (2) of ourselves not able to free us out of bondage: that there was no means to set us at liberty, but the most precious ransom, which Christ our blessed Saviour paid for us. (3) That we should acknow- the infinite love of God [a] the Father, who gave his Son, and of the Son [b] who gave himself to be a ransom for us. (4) That we may acknowledge ourselves bound to be thankful [c] unto him, for "let them give thanks whom the Lord hath redeemed." (5) That we may highly esteem of this liberty, which cost so dear a price: that with all diligence we use the means to obtain it, and never be at rest until we be made partakers of it: when we have obtained it, to [d] stand fast in it; not to abuse it to licentiousness, but to use it to the glory of our Redeemer, who hath freed us from the spiritual bondage of sin and Satan, not that we might sin freely, but that we might "[e] serve God without fear, in holiness and righteousness before him all the days of our life." We must remember, that being [f] bought with a price, we are not our own, but his that bought us: and therefore should not seek

The key truth that unlocks the door to freedom.

a John iii. 16; 1 John iv. 10. b John xv. 13.
c Psalm cvii. 2; Col. i. 12, 13, 14; Rom. vii. 25; 1 Cor. xv. 57. d Galat. v. 1. e Luke i. 74.
f 1 Cor. vi. 19, 20.

ourselves, or serve our own lusts, but should glorify him both in our souls and bodies, which are not ours, but his that hath bought us, &c. and so much of the author of this liberty.

Sect. 5. The subject of this liberty, or parties on whom it is conferred.

Now followeth the subject or parties to whom this liberty belongeth, which by the context appeareth to be those, who by the grace of adoption and regeneration, are made the sons of God in Christ. For naturally we are all servants, serving a most servile and slavish servitude under sin and Satan; which must seriously be acknowledged of us, before we will either truly desire to be made partakers of this liberty, (for none need to be freed, but those that are in bondage) or will profit by this doctrine, as appertaining unto us. Our Saviour therefore, according to the[a] prophesy of Isaiah, saith,[b] that he was sent to " preach liberty and deliverance to the captives." and " to set at liberty the broken hearted." He came to seek and to " save[c] that which was lost :" neither came he to[d] " call the righteous (in their own conceits) but sinners unto repentance :" to fill the[e] poor and the hungry[f] with good things, whilst the rich are sent empty away.

a Isaiah lxi i. b Luke iv. 18. c Matt. xviii. 11.
d Matt. ix. 13. e Matt. v. 3, 6. f Luke i. 53.

Neither must we deceive ourselves with this conceit, that because we profess ourselves to be redeemed; and do live in the house of God which is his visible Church, therefore we have all attained this liberty already. For, in the house of God, there be as well [g] vessels of dishonour, as vessels of honour; in the [h] floor of God, as well chaff as wheat; in the [i] net of God, as well bad fish as that which is good; in the [k] field of God, as well tares as corn; in the family or house of God, as well [l] servants as sons; in the flock of God, as well [m] goats as sheep. Unless therefore you be the sons of God by faith, truly called, engrafted into Christ as his members, regenerated by the Spirit of God, this liberty as yet doth not belong unto you. For it is a liberty, as the Apostle saith, "[n] which we have in Christ," that is, which we being in Christ have by him, as after we shall hear: (which also) is conferred upon us, in and by our vocation, justification, and sanctification; and therefore none enjoy it, as actually made free, but such as are sanctified, justified, and called.

But here some will object: are not we the Church of God, and is not the church a company of men called? have we not been

g 2 Tim. ii. 20. h Matt. iii. 12. i Matt. xiii. 47.
k Matt. xiii. 24. l John viii. 34, 35
m Matt. xxv. 32, 33. n Galat. ii. 4

baptized, and by baptism regenerated, made the members of Christ, and children of God? How then do you say, we are not free? Beloved, as this objection is not unlike the cavil of the captious Jews in this place; so must it receive the like answer. "Verily, verily, I say unto you," saith our Saviour, "he that committeth sin is the servant of sin, and the servant shall not abide in the house," &c. I know that you are the Church of God, as these Jews were; and that you have been baptized, as they had been circumcised. But you must distinguish, first, of the Church; that there is a Church visible, and a Church invisible, which is the mystical body of Christ. And you are to know, that there be many in the Church visible, which are not[o] of the Church invisible; many in the house of God, which be servants and not sons. Secondly, of calling; that there is an outward calling by the Word, which is common to all in the Church, of which it is said, [p] many be called, and few chosen. And there is an inward and effectual calling, according to God's *purpose*, of which it is said, [q] whom he elected, he called. Thirdly, of Baptism; there is an outward Baptism, which is the sprinkling of the [r] flesh with water, and an inward Baptism, wherein the soul is

o 1 John ii. 19. p Matt. xx. 16. and xxii. 14.
q Rom. viii. 28, 30. r 1 Peter iii. 21.

[s] sprinkled with the blood of Christ, and with the water of the Holy Ghost, whereof the outward is a sign. Fourthly, of union with Christ, for there is a sacramental union in Baptism, and a spiritual by the [t] Holy Ghost and by faith. Lastly, of Christians, members of Christ, sons of God. For as the Apostle distinguisheth the [u] Jews, that they were either outwardly Jews and in shew, or inwardly and in truth; and our Saviour in the next [x] words, the seed of *Abraham* according to the flesh, and according to the promise. For, as *Paul* also saith, " they [y] which be of faith, are the sons of Abraham:" so men are called Christians, members of Christ, sons of God, not only who are such in deed and in truth; but also such as are Christians only in profession, members of Christ in appearance, [z] sons of God in respect of the outward covenant. Wherefore though you live in the visible Church, though you be called, though you have been baptized, and by baptism sacramentally united to the body of Christ, which is his Church; though in your own profession, and in the reputation of others, who conceive of you (as they ought) according to the judgment of charity, you are Christians, members of Christ, and sons of the kingdom: notwithstanding, if you do not

s Heb xii 24. t 1 Cor. xii. 13. u Rom. ii. 28, 29.
x John viii. 37, &c. y Gal. iii. 7.
z Ezek. xvi. 20, 21. ; Matt. viii. 12.

Judgement is JUST — for we are without excuse if we REJECT Salvation in Ch
It would be better—That we HADN'T heard!

truly believe in Christ and unfeignedly repent of your sins, you are servants and not sons. Yea, so far shall these outward privileges be from exempting you from damnation, that they shall greatly aggravate your judgment. For hath God called us, and we are not called? hath he invited us to turn unto him, and we are not converted? hath he by his ministers [a] intreated us, that we would be reconciled unto him, and we will not be reconciled? hath he offered us infinite mercy in the mystery of our salvation by Christ, and we have despised the same, not caring to apprehend the mercies of God and merits of Christ, but suffering his precious blood to be spilt as it were on the ground in vain? hath he often sought [b] to gather us unto him, as the hen gathered the chickens under her wings, and we would not? Then have the means of salvation been the means of obduration unto us; and the word, which to the faithful, is the [c] savour of life unto life, unto us is become a savour of death unto death. Yea, for this contempt of the Gospel, if we persist in it, our estate in the day of judgment shall be more [d] intolerable, than theirs of Sodom and Gomorrah. And unto us belongeth that fearful woe denounced by our Saviour Christ, [e] Woe to thee Bethsaida, Woe to

a 2 Cor. v. 20. b Matt. xxiii. 37. c 2 Cor. ii. 16.
d Matt. x. 15. e Matt. xi. 21, 23.

The sad realities of condemnation & slavery for the unregenerate, who place so much faith in "the church."

thee Capernaum: for if the means which you have had, had been vouchsafed to them of Tyrus and Sidon, yea, to them of Sodom, they would have turned unto God, but "I say unto you, it shall be easier for them in the day of judgment, than for you." Again, hath the Lord sent his Son to redeem us, given us means to apply Christ unto us; hath he entreated us to believe and repent, and put to his seal in baptism, thereby assuring us, that if we believe and repent, our souls are washed with the blood of Christ, that we are ingrafted into him, and in him are made the sons of God, and heirs of eternal life? Shall not we therefore most worthily perish in our sins, if notwithstanding we will not believe and repent; especially having in our baptism by a solemn vow bound ourselves thereto. The consideration whereof must force men, who are not yet regenerated, unfeignedly to turn unto God, and to lay hold upon Christ by faith. For it is most certain, though they live in the house of God, which is his Church, yet until they truly believe and repent, they are servants and not sons: and such servants as are held under the most miserable and basest slavery of sin and Satan: being not only bound hand and foot, yea in heart and mind, so that they can neither do nor think that which is spiritually good; but are also carried away [f] captive, to perform

f 2 Tim. ii. 26.; Titus iii. 3.

the will of Satan, and the lusts of the flesh; whereby it comes to pass, that as they can do no good, so can they do nothing but sin.

Sect. 6. The quality or property of this liberty.

The next thing to be considered is, the quality of this liberty, viz. that it is a true liberty. For neither is it an imaginary liberty, as in the paradox of the Stoics, who held that wise men of the world were only free, when they also, being not freed by Christ, were and are no better but servants; or in the secure imaginations of carnal men, who with these Jews, though being in bondage, think themselves free. Neither is it a loose liberty or licentiousness, such as libertines assume to themselves, but a true and a holy liberty, whereby we, being freed from sin, become servants of righteousness, and being delivered from the hands of our spiritual enemies, are enabled to worship God with willing minds and cheerful hearts; for that is the only true liberty: and such is the liberty of the Saints in Heaven, and of the blessed Angels, who count it not only their liberty, but also their happiness, willingly and cheerfully to serve the Lord. For if the Son, who is the truth, shall make you free, then shall you be free ὄντως, in deed and in truth.

This, therefore, as it serveth for the comfort of the godly; so also for the terror of the wicked: for, from this speech of our Saviour, we may conclude both ways. 1. Whosoever are made free by Christ they are free indeed; but all the faithful are made free by Christ; therefore, (whatsoever the devil or their own corruption can object to the contrary,) they are free indeed.

Again, if the Son make you free, saith Christ, then are you free indeed; but you, (say I to unbelievers and impenitent sinners,) are not free indeed: "for he that committeth sin is the servant of sin;" therefore, howsoever you profess yourselves redeemed by Christ, and howsoever, also, it be most true, that Christ hath paid a ransom sufficient for the redemption of all; yet are you not actually redeemed, nor the benefit of redemption applied unto you, until you be ingrafted into Christ by faith, and renewed by the Holy Ghost. And the same may be confirmed by the oath of the Lord, "wherein[a] it is impossible that he should lie;" the oath which he sware to our father Abraham, that he would give us, both that we should be delivered from the hand, that is, the power and dominion of our spiritual enemies; and[b] being "delivered, should also have grace to worship God without fear, in holiness and righteousness before him, all the days of our life." If, therefore, we do not endeavour to

a Heb. vi. 18. b Luke i. 73, 74.

worship God in holiness and righteousness, with willing minds and upright hearts, it is as sure as the oath of the Lord is true, that as yet we are not actually freed and redeemed by Christ. For, "if the Son make you free, you shall be free indeed."

And thus much of the general doctrine of Christian liberty, wherein I have been the shorter, because all these points, whereof I have thus generally and briefly spoken, viz. that Christian liberty is a spiritual liberty which the faithful have in and by Christ Jesus; that it consisteth on two parts, an immunity and freedom from all spiritual bondage, and an ἐξȣσία and right to the privileges and liberties of God's children: that Christ our redeemer is the author of this liberty, both in respect of his merit and efficacy; that it is bestowed only upon the faithful, who are the sons of God and members of Christ: and lastly, that this liberty of Christians is a true liberty; all these points, I say, will more plainly and fully appear in the particulars, whereunto we are now to descend.

Sect. 7. The special doctrine of Christian liberty.

Viæ, of this life, such as is incident unto us while we are in the way, whereof[a] some not unfitly understand our Saviour

a Luke xii. 58.

The Special Doctrine of Christian freedom is in 2 parts:
1. Redemption – making us HEIRS – in hope + expectation – the 'not yet' but 'already' of the Kingdom of God – The Liberty of GRACE – Eph. 1.7-14.
2. Redemption of POSSESSION – in deed + possession – perfect, complete freedom IN CHRIST – The Liberty of GLORY Rom 8.21.

Christian liberty therefore is either *libertas*

to speak, Luke xii. 58. "Give diligence to be delivered from thy adversary, while thou art in the way," &c. understanding by the Governor, God; by the Judge, Christ; by the adversary, the devil, sin, a guilty conscience, the sentence of the law; by the way, this life; by the officer, the Angels; by prison, hell, &c.

Patriæ, of the life to come, which we shall enjoy, when being come to the end of our way, we shall have the [b] end of our faith, which is the salvation of our souls.

The former is freedom from the bondage of sin, the other from the bondage [c] of corruption. The former is simply called ἀπολύτρωσις,[d] redemption, the latter ἀπολύτρωσις της περιποιήσεως, the redemption of possession: for by the former we are heirs, *spe*, in hope and expectation; by the latter, *re*, in deed and possession; the one is begun and in part, the other perfect and complete: the one the liberty of grace, the other, as the Apostle speaketh, [e] ἐλευθερία τῆς δόξης, "the liberty of glory."

b 1 Pet. i. 9. c Rom viii. 21.
d Eph. i. 7—14. e Rom. viii. 21.

Freedom is common to the faithful in both Old and New Testaments — but there is a difference between pre-Incarnation tutoring / governance and post Incarnation liberty IN CHRIST — though the same FAITH is effectual in both.

The liberty of grace.

Of these in order: And first, of the liberty of grace, which even in this life the faithful do enjoy in and by Christ. And it is either common to all the faithful, as well of the old Testament as of the new; or peculiar to the faithful under the Gospel. The faithful under both Testaments were and are sons; who as they have the same [f] common faith; so have they the same [g] common salvation, and therefore the same liberty and right, in respect of the inheritance itself, and all the degrees thereof. Notwithstanding there is difference between sons under age, and in their minority, in respect of discipline and government, and those who are come to years: the former being nurtured by schoolmasters, and governed by tutors, as the Apostle saith [h] of the faithful before the incarnation of Christ; the latter set at liberty from such discipline and government. Otherwise, as they had the same faith, and the same justification (for all the faithful both before Christ and after, were and are justified by faith, as Abraham [i] was, Rom. iv. and by such [k] a faith, James ii.) so have they the same liberty which is obtained by faith, and in some chief points thereof is, as [l] Calvin saith, an appendix of justification.

f Titus i. 4. g Jude iii.
h Gal. iv. 2, 3, & 3—24. i Rom. iv. 23, 24.
k Jam. ii. 20, 21. l Instit. lib.3. cap. 19. § 1.

The liberty of saving grace. The common liberty of grace, which may fitly be called the liberty of saving grace, containeth many particulars; which, for your easier remembrance, may be reduced to these three heads.

For it is a liberty which we have in and by our { Vocation. / Justification. / Sanctification. }

For, although these three concur in time, because a man is no sooner effectually called, but he is also justified before God, and no sooner justified, but he beginneth also to be sanctified (which is duly to be observed of those, who presuming, and that perhaps for a long time, that they be called and justified, do still remain unsanctified) notwithstanding in order of nature [m] vocation goeth before justification, and justification before sanctification. And let this also by the way be observed for the comfort of the godly. For whosoever, professing the true faith, hath a true purpose and unfeigned desire to walk before God in the obedience of his will, making conscience of all his ways: that man, howsoever besides his general purpose he may fail ([n] as we all do) in many particulars; yet he is sanctified, and from his sanctification may certainly conclude, that he is justified, that he is called, that he is elected, that

m Rom. viii. 30. n Jam. iii. 2.

The Liberty of VOCATION: 1. Our MINDS are freed, enlightened, persuaded
2. Our HEARTS are softened
3. Our WILLS are inspired. - NOT compelled to come and to follow Christ.
See Summary p. 33 and Conclusion pp 35-36

he shall be saved. For the fruit could not be good, unless the tree or the branch that beareth it were good, and the branch cannot be good, unless it be ingrafted into Christ,[o] the only true vine: that is to say, a man's conversation is never acceptable unto God, before his person be accepted; and his person is not accepted, until he be united unto Christ. For the better understanding of this point, we must remember, that Christ at a dear price hath long since purchased this liberty for us, and hath meritoriously wrought our freedom. But none are actually and effectually set at liberty, but those alone, who have actual union and communion with Christ. Now in our effectual vocation, we have union with Christ; and in our justification and sanctification, communion with him. In the former, in respect of his merits apprehended by faith, and communicated unto us by imputation; in the other, in respect of his graces, which being in him without measure, are by his spirit from[p] him derived, and in some measure communicated unto us by infusion.

Sect. 8. *The liberty of vocation.*

But let us speak of them severally. And first, as touching our vocation, I say with the Apostle,[a] Gal. v. "Brethren,

o John xv. 1. 5. p John i. 16. a Gal. v. 12.

you are called unto liberty;" which words we are thus to understand, that by our calling we are not only invited unto Christian liberty in general, as a main benefit of our Christian profession; but also by it are enfranchised, being thereby put into possession of a good part of it, and entitled to the rest. For whereas naturally we are wholly, and not only in part (for that may be verified of the faithful, Rom. vii. 14.) carnal, sold under sin; by our calling we are first made spiritual, being in some measure indued with the spirit of Christ. Now the spirit of Christ being the spirit of liberty, as David speaketh, [b] Psalm li. we may resolve with the Apostle, [c] that "where the spirit of the Lord is there is liberty."

But the liberty which we have by our calling standeth on these degrees. First, as it is as an immunity; our minds are therein free from the servitude of blindness and incredulity, our hearts and wills from the bondage of that which the Apostle calleth [d] ἀπείθειαν (under which all men naturally are concluded) that is, disobedience and infidelity; ourselves, from the servitude of Satan becalled, and as it were culled out of the world, whereby is meant the company of worldly men, which is the kingdom of the devil, (who is the [e] prince, yea the God [f] of the

b Ps. li. 14. c 2 Cor. iii. 17.
d Rom. xi. 32. e John xii. 31. f 2 Cor. iv. 4.

world, working effectually ἐν τοῖς υἱοῖς τῆς ἀπειθείας, [g] in the children of infidelity and disobedience, blinding their understandings and [h] captivating their wills:) and lastly, translated from the most slavish state of damnation, being [i] redeemed from among men, and delivered out of the [k] world, which because it wholly, as St. John saith,[l] ἐν τω πονηρῷ κεῖται, lieth under the subjection of the devil, (who hath the [m] power of death) is also subject to death and damnation.

As it is ἐξουσία, that is, a power and interest, we are in our calling endued, as I said, with the spirit of liberty, which freeth our souls by enlightening our minds, persuading our judgments, and softening our hearts, inspiring thereinto godly desires and gracious resolutions, whereby he beginning the grace of faith in us, doth regenerate us and unite us unto Christ. So that by our effectual calling, in regard that therein the spirit of liberty is communicated unto us, and the saving grace of faith is therein begotten in us, we are made the sons of God and members of Christ, and are not only entitled to all the rights and privileges of the children of God and members of Christ;

g Eph. ii, 2. h 2 Tim. ii. 26
i Apoc. xiv. 4. k Gal. i. 4. l 1 John v. 19.
For he is ὁ πονηρὸς of whom he had spoken, Ver. 18.
m Heb. ii. 15.

but also are presently [n] translated, as it were, from death to life, and from a state of damnation unto the state of grace and salvation.

But these things do need some further explanation. First, therefore, in the ministry of the gospel, which is the ministry [o] of the Spirit, the word [p] of faith, the seed of regeneration, the [q] law or doctrine of liberty, and the ordinary means of our [r] vocation, the Lord preventing us with his grace, sendeth the Spirit of his Son into our hearts, which being, as I said, the spirit of liberty; first, freeth our minds from the bondage of ignorance, incredulity and vanity, wherein until then we are held captive, not once able of ourselves to entertain a [s] good thought, the whole frame of our thoughts being [t] only evil continually; the wisdom of our flesh [u], or that which our flesh mindeth, being enmity against God, ourselves not only not perceiving, but being [v] not able to perceive the things which are of the Spirit of God, and much less able to give assent unto them (for no man can say that [w] Jesus is Christ but the Holy Ghost) and much less to assent effectually, or by a lively faith. The Spirit of God, therefore, by the ministry of the

n John v. 24. o 2 Cor. iii. 8. 1 Pet. i. 23.
p Rom. x. 8. q Jam. i. 18. 25. r 2 Thes. ii. 14.
s 2 Cor. iii. 5. t Gen. vi. 5. and viii. 21.
u Rom. viii, 7. v 1 Cor. ii. 14. w 1 Cor. xii. 3.

word (which is a [x] light unto our feet) as the means, and by the ministers of the gospel, as his instruments (who are therefore called the [y] light of the world, and are sent by Christ to [z] open our eyes, and to give light to them that sit in [a] darkness, and in the shadow of death) enlighteneth our minds to understand, and openeth our hearts as he did the heart of Lydia, persuading our souls [b] *προσέχειν τοῖς λαλεμένοις*, that is, not only to attend, but as the word also signifieth, to assent to those things which are spoken by the ministers; and thereby maketh us unfeignedly to acknowledge and seriously to consider, both our miserable servitude, and damnable estate in ourselves, and also the gracious liberty and saving grace of God offered in Christ. And this is the first degree of the liberty which we have in our calling, that therein we are called out [c] of darkness into light. Of this liberty the apostle speaketh, 2 Cor. iii. [d] that whereas there is naturally a veil over men's hearts, that they cannot understand the word; this veil is taken away by the Spirit of God, when they turn unto the Lord. Now the Lord (saith he) "is the Spirit, and where the Spirit of the Lord is there is liberty."

x Psalm cxix, 105.
y Matt. v. 14.
z Acts xxvi. 18.
a Luke i. 79.
b Acts xvi. 14.
c 1 Pet. ii. 9.
d 2 Cor. iii. 15, 16, 17.

In this regard the Spirit is compared to an [d] eye-salve, and is called that [e] anointing, which, being received from Christ, teacheth us all things.

Having thus revealed unto us both our own miserable estate in ourselves, and the infinite mercies of God in Christ, and moved us truly to assent thereto; in the next place he toucheth our hearts with a sense of our misery, and with a hatred of sin, which hath brought us into that miserable estate, and by the ministry of the word, which is his [f] power, to our salvation, and his arm [g] to draw us unto him, he turneth our will and affections from darkness (which naturally [h] we love) unto light, not only working in us hearty desires to come out of that damnable estate, and to be made partakers of Christ (which desires also he being the [i] Spirit of Supplication, helpeth us to express in hearty prayer;) but also inspiring into us a settled resolution, that for as much as liberty and salvation is promised to all that receive Christ by faith; we will therefore resolve undoubtedly to acknowledge him to be our only Saviour, and to rest upon him alone for salvation. Thus by working, 1. In our minds an effectual assent to the promise of the Gospel. 2. In our hearts an earnest de-

d Apoc iii. 18. e 1 John ii. 27, f Rom. i. 16.
g Is. liii. 1. h John iii. 19. Acts xxvi. 18.
i Zech. xii. 10. Rom. viii. 26.

sire to be made partakers of Christ's merits; and (3) In our will a settled resolution to acknowledge him to be the Messiah, and to rely upon the mercies of God and the merits of Christ for justification and salvation, (by which three we do [k] receive Christ,) the Spirit of God begetteth the grace of justifying faith in us. In the begetting whereof, he doth not only [l] turn men from darkness to light, and from the power of Satan unto God, but also regenerateth them and uniteth them unto Christ, making them of the children of wrath the sons of God, of the imps of the old Adam, members of Christ, and of the subjects of Satan in the kingdom of [m] darkness fellow [n] citizens with the saints in the kingdom of God. And this is the liberty which we have by our calling. As for the teachers of free will, and the magnifiers of our pure naturals, they neither acknowledge the woeful bondage wherein we are by nature, nor the happy liberty whereunto we are not born but called. For this is a liberty, *ad quam non nati, sed renati sumus*, which we have not by generation, but by regeneration. Neither is it a common liberty of all, but a liberty peculiar to the people of God, who are a people [o] set at liberty, peculiar to the sons of God and members of Christ. But

k John i. 12. l Acts xxvi. 18. m Col. i 13.
n Eph. ii. 19. o 1 Pet. ii. 9.

it will be said, if there be no freedom in our wills before we be called, then belike we are called and saved against our wills, and we must look with the enthusiasts for violent raptures. I answer, that there is in our will a freedom of nature, whereby it is free from compulsion. For, that the will should be forced it implieth a contradiction, for then it should both will and nill the same thing at one time. Notwithstanding this freedom of the will, until it be freed by grace, is a voluntary service of sin; voluntarily and with greediness, willing that which is evil, although it can will nothing else. But the preventing grace of God whereby we are called is persuasive; drawing us indeed, and so of unwilling making us willing, but this is by persuasion and not by compulsion. For although our wills in the first act of our conversion be merely passive, and none can come to Christ unless the [p] Father draw him, yet we can no sooner conceive a man to be effectually called, than that he is made willing. For in the very act of our calling, of unwilling we are made willing, and no sooner are we effectually drawn but we willingly come; in which sense true is that saying of Chrysostom, *ἕλκοι μεν ὁ ϑεὸς, βουλόμενον δὲ ἕλκει,* God indeed draweth, but he draweth him that is

p John vi. 44.

willing. Wherefore though our wills do not concur, *ad vocationem,* unto our calling, yet they concur, *in vocatione,* in our calling, being therein made free.

Sect. 9. Justification and sanctification not to be confounded.

Now we are to entreat of the liberty which we have both in our justification, and also in our sanctification. For, howsoever these graces do always so concur, as that whosoever hath the one, hath the other; and whosoever hath not both, hath neither; yet are we carefully to distinguish them. For the Papists in not distinguishing them, confound the law and the Gospel, abolish the main benefit of Christ, which in the Scriptures goeth under the name of justification, and with it the liberty which we have by it; and lastly, by their Antichristian doctrine teach men to place the matter of their justification, and the merit of salvation in themselves. For they do teach, that a man is justified, when he is made righteous by righteousness inherent in himself, and performed by himself, and accordingly make two degrees of justification: the one, which they call the first justification, when a man of a sinner is made just, by the infusion of faith, hope, and charity; the other, which they call the second justification, when a man of a just man is made more just by bringing forth good works. So that according to their doctrine, the righteousness of the first justification, is habitual and inherent in themselves; of the second, actual, and performed by themselves. And whereas justification standeth on two parts, viz. remission of sin, and the making, or, as the[a] Apostle speaketh, constituting of us righteous; as they teach, that we are made righteous, not by imputation, but by infusion of righteousness: so they teach, that remission of sin is the deletion of sin, and that sins are then pardoned, when by infusion of the contrary graces they are expelled. Even as water is then said to be warmed, when by the accession of heat the cold is expelled. Again, where the Scripture saith,[b] that we are justified by grace, that is, by the mere favour of God in Christ, by faith without works, by the righteousness of God, which, without the law is manifested in the Gospel; they by grace understand the graces of God in us, which they say concur with faith unto justification; by righteousness, not the righteousness of Christ apprehended by faith, but a righteousness from Christ infused into us, &c. Which doctrines, being understood of sanctification, are for the most part true. For we do not deny, but that the matter of our sanctification is inherent in us, and

a Rom. v. 19. b Rom. iii. 24.

performed by us; and that it is partly habitual, and partly actual: that it consisteth in our dying unto sin, which is called mortification, and living unto righteousness, which is called vivification: that there be degrees thereof, according to the measure of grace received: that we are sanctified by the grace, or rather graces of God in us; and that thereunto not faith alone, but hope and charity, and other both inward graces and outward obedience do concur, &c.

But if the justification, which the Papists teach, be nothing else but sanctification; what then is become of that, which in the Scriptures goeth under the name of justification, and is the main benefit of the Messiah, whereby we are not only freed from the guilt of sin, which bound us over to death and damnation; but also are in Christ accepted as righteous, and made heirs of eternal life: by which we are freed from the fear of damnation, and are entitled unto the kingdom of heaven: surely by the Popish doctrine it is in a manner abolished, and with it the liberty which we have by it, which is no less than our deliverance from hell, and our title to the kingdom of heaven, which, if we have not by Christ, we have no salvation by him. For it is certain, that whereby we are justified, thereby we are saved.

This most pernicious and Antichristian error they seek to justify by the like notation of the Latin words. For as to be sanctified, is to be made holy, by holiness wrought in us; so to be justified, in their conceit, is to be made just, by righteousness wrought in us.

Whereunto I answer, that if the Latin notation were to be respected, it would not hinder our cause. For, we do freely confess, that whom the Lord justifieth, he maketh just. But then the question is, whether by imputation, or by infusion. By imputation, we say, as he justifieth; by infusion, not as he justifieth, but as he sanctifieth. But the Latin word is no farther to be urged, than as it is the translation of the Hebrew word in the Old Testament, and of the Greek in the New, which signifieth to justify. Now, it is plain, that both the Hebrew הצדיק, and the Greek δικαιȣν, is *verbum forense*, a judicial word ascribed unto God, as the Judge; to teach us, when we think of justification, to summon ourselves before the judgment seat of God. And in this sense it is opposed to condemning, as in the [c] judgments of men, Deut. xxv. 1; Prov. xvii. 15, so in the [d] judgment of God, Matt. xii. 37. By thy words thou shalt be justified, and by thy words thou shalt be condemned; 1 Kings viii. 32; Rom. v. 16, 18; and Rom. viii. 33.[e] Hereby

c Deut. xxv. 1; Prov. xvii. 15. d Matt. xii. 37.
e 1 Kings viii. 32; Rom. v. 16, 18; Rom. viii. 33.

then appeareth, both what justification is, and wherein it differeth from sanctification. For the contrary to justifying is polluting, but the contrary to sanctifying, is condemning. Wherefore as sanctifying being the contrary to polluting, doth signify making holy; so justifying being the contrary to condemning, doth signify absolving, acquitting, pronouncing just. And in this sense evermore, in the question of justification, it is used when it is ascribed unto God. Neither are the Papists able to produce any one testimony, where justification being ascribed to God, (as[f] It is God that doth justify) doth signify making righteous by infusion. This then is the first note of difference, whereunto others may be added. For in justification, as I said before, we have communion with Christ, in respect of his merits imputed unto us, to free us from the guilt of sin, and fear of damnation, and to entitle us to the kingdom of heaven. In sanctification we have communion with Christ in respect of his graces, which being in him without measure, are by his Spirit derived to us in measure, and communicated by infusion, to free us from the corruption and dominion of sin, and to prepare and fit us for the kingdom of heaven.

The matter therefore of justification, or

f Rom. iii. 26, and viii. 33.

that whereby we are absolved, and in respect whereof, God doth acquit us from our sins, and accepting us as just, doth so pronounce of us, is the merits, righteousness, and obedience of Christ our Saviour. For by what we are redeemed, by that we have [g] remission of sins, or justification; but we are redeemed only by the merits and righteousness of Christ, and not by our own; and therefore we are justified by the righteousness of Christ, and not by that which is inherent in us, or performed by us: but our sanctification consisteth in the graces of God's Spirit inherent in us, and the new obedience performed by us.

We are justified by imputation of Christ's righteousness, when God imputing to a believer the righteousness of Christ, and accepting of it in the believer's behalf, as if he had performed it in his own person, doth not only acquit him from his sins, but also accepteth of him as righteous in Christ, and as an heir of eternal life. For as Christ was made a sinner for us, so are we made [h] righteous before God in him: Christ was made a sinner for us, by imputation of our sins to him: therefore we are made righteous before God in him, by imputation of his righteousness unto us. Again, as we were made sinners, that is, guilty of the first

g Ephes. i. 7; Colos. i. 14.
h 2 Cor. v. 21.

Adam's transgression;[i] so are we justified by the obedience of the second Adam. But we are guilty of the first Adam's transgression by imputation. For how should that being an action, and therefore transient, be communicated unto us? Let Bellarmine answer: It is communicated to us, saith he,[k] as transient things used to be communicated, that is to say, *by imputation.* Therefore we are justified by imputation of the obedience of the second Adam. For the obedience of Christ, which he performed on earth, being transient, how could it be communicated unto us, but as Bellarmine saith, all transient things are communicated, viz. by imputation. The reason of which imputation is this. For as all men being in Adam as the root of mankind, originally, are guilty of his sin, it being imputed unto them, because in him and by him, by reason of their union with him, all sinned: so the faithful being in Christ as their head or root, are justified by his obedience, it being imputed to them, because in him, and by him, by

i Rom. v. 18. 9.

k Adæ peccatum nobis communicatur per generationem eo modo, quo communicari potest id quod transit, nimirum per imputationem. Omnibus enim imputatur, qui ex Adamo nascuntur, quoniam omnes in lumbis Adami existentes, in ei et per cum peccavimus, cum ipse peccavit. Bellarm. tom. 3. de amiss. grat. et stat. pec. lib. 5, cap. 17.

reason of our union with him, we fulfilled the law, and in him, and by him we satisfied the justice of God. But we are sanctified by the infusion of grace wrought in us by the Holy Ghost.

Justification is the very entitling of us to the kingdom of heaven. Sanctification is both the badge and cognizance, whereby they are to be discerned and known who are justified, and shall be[1] saved, and the fitting and preparing of us to that kingdom, whereinto no unclean thing shall enter.

The righteousness of justification is perfect; (for it is the righteousness of Christ,) and therefore of justification itself there are no degrees, though of the assurance thereof there be degrees, according to the measure of faith. The righteousness of our sanctification, which is inherent, is unperfect in this life, and stained with the flesh; and thereof there are degrees, as we grow in grace.

We are both justified and sanctified by faith, but in divers respects. We are justified by faith, because by it we apprehend the righteousness of Christ, and therefore are justified by it, not formally, as it is a power or habit in us, or as it is a part of inherent righteousness, but relatively in respect of the object which it doth apprehend; and by it

1 Acts xxvi. 18, and xx. 32.

alone we are justified, because it is the only grace in us, which apprehendeth the merits of Christ to justification. We are sanctified by faith, as a chief part of our sanctification, being as it were the root, both of other inward graces, and outward obedience: but we are not sanctified by it alone, because not only other graces inherent, but also outward obedience concur thereto.

Sect. 10. The liberty of justification. These things thus premised, let us consider what that liberty is, which we have both in our justification, and also in our sanctification. In both (as our freedom is an immunity) we are freed from sin, and from the law, which is the strength of sin, though in different respects, which will be so many more differences betwixt justification and sanctification. In sin there are two things, the guilt thereof, and the corruption. In justification we are freed wholly from the guilt of sin: for to be justified, is to have remission of sin, [a] Rom. iv. 6, 7, or which is all one, to be freed, or absolved from the guilt of it.

Freedom from guilt of sin. And so certain it is, that in justification we have this freedom, that to be justified, is to be freed, according to the Scriptures phrase,[b] Rom. vi. 7., "he that is dead is freed from sin:" the Greek is δεδικαίωται, see[c] Acts xiii. 38, 39. "Be it

a Rom. iv. 6, 7. b Rom. vi. 7. c Acts xiii. 38, 39.

known unto you, that through Christ is preached unto us forgiveness of sins. And from all things, from which you could not be justified by the law of Moses, by him every one that believeth is justified. Where, to be justified, is to have pardon of sin, or freedom from the guilt of it."

The guilt of sin is the obligation of binding over of the sinner unto punishment: and this bond is partly in the law,[d] which is the handwriting or obligation that is against us, binding over the transgressor of it, to the punishment threatened in it; and partly in the [e] conscience, applying the law, moral or natural, to the sinner, and from thence [f] pronouncing him subject to punishment. From this obligation or guilt we are freed before God, and as it were in the court of heaven, so soon as we believe: and we are freed from the same in the court of conscience, when we know that we believe, and are assured of our justification. For, [g] by faith we have remission of sin; and whosoever [h] believeth in Christ, he is justified from the guilt thereof.

This our freedom containeth in it happiness, for as their estate is miserable, whose sins are not forgiven, because by their sins they are

d As the συντήρησις, or proposition.
e συνείδησις, or assumption.
f κριτήριον, or conclusion.
g Acts xxvi. 18. h Acts xiii. 38, 39.

debtors unto God, owing in respect thereof eternal death and damnation (though they only feel this burthen, whose conscience is thoroughly touched, of whom it is aid, [i] a wounded spirit who is able to bear?) so their estate is happy, who are freed from the guilt of sin. *David*, though a king, flourishing in great honour, wealth, and delights; notwithstanding he reposeth his felicity in the forgiveness of sin, [k] Psalm xxxii. "Blessed is the man whose wickedness is forgiven, and whose sin is covered, blessed is the man to whom the Lord imputeth not iniquity."— Which should move us above all things to labour for the forgiveness of sin, and for the assurance thereof. If thou believe in Christ, and withal confess thy sin [l] and forsake [m] it, thou must be sure that it is pardoned.

Sec. 11. Freedom from the Law.

Secondly, in our justification we are freed from the [a] law, and that in two respects. First, from the malediction or condemnation of it: secondly, from the law's exaction of inherent and that perfect righteousness unto justification. Under which double yoke of bondage all men are, that are not justified by faith in Christ: that is, all men in themselves are subject to the curse [b] who

i Prov. xviii. 14. k Psalm xxxii. 1, 2; Rom. iv. 6.
l 1 John i. 9. m Prov. xxviii. 13. a Gal. iv. 4, 5.
b Gal. iii. 10.

in the least degree do at any time in their whole life transgress any part of the law, as all men oftentimes do; and again, no man who is not in Christ, can be exempted from the curse, and attain to justification, unless he continue in all the things which are written in the book of the law to do them; which no man is able to do, the law by reason of the flesh being [c] impossible unto us. Let natural or unconverted men apply this to themselves. Canst thou not by the sentence of the law be exempted from the curse, unless thou dost not only not commit the things forbidden, but also do the duties commanded; unless thou dost all, and unless thou continuest in doing all, never failing in any one particular; and finally, unless thou continuest in doing all, and every thing commanded in that perfect manner and measure which the law prescribeth? Alas then, how wilt thou escape the dreadful curse, who instead of doing the duties commanded, hast done the vices forbidden; who instead of keeping all the commandments, hast broken them all; and instead of continuing in a total, perpetual, and perfect obedience of the law, hast continued in the disobedience thereof? Hence we may conclude with the Apostle, that all men in themselves, even those [d] who seek to be justified by the law, be concluded under sin, and consequently under the curse: and

c Rom. viii. 3. d Gal. iii. 10.

therefore have extreme need to seek unto Christ, that by him they may be set free from this two-fold bondage; which is, to be under the curse of the law if we break it, when we can do nothing else but break it; and to be excluded from justification, if we do not continue in the perfect performance of the law, when we are not able so much as to [e] think a good thought, or once to will that which is spiritually good. But by Christ we are freed from both. First, from the curse, as the Apostle in express terms teacheth: "[f] Christ hath redeemed us from the curse of the law, when he was made a curse for us." He hath freed us from the punishment of sin, by undergoing the punishment for us, he hath acquitted us from our debts by discharging them for us. For as *Isaiah* [g] saith, "He was wounded for our transgressions, he was broken for our iniquities, the chastisement of our peace (that is, which was to procure us peace and reconciliation with God) was laid upon him," and "by his stripes we are healed." And again, "[h] The Lord hath laid upon him the iniquity of us all," that is, the punishment of all our sins. And, "[i] My righteous servant by his knowledge," that is, by the knowledge of him, or faith in him, "shall justify many, for he shall bear their iniquities."

Freedom from the curse of the Law.

e 2 Cor. iv. 5. f Gal. iii. 13. g Isa. liii. 3.
h Isa. liii. 6. i Ibid. ver. xi.

Now, by the curse of the law from which Christ doth free us, we are to understand all evil [k] of punishment, as well temporal as eternal: for it is absurd to imagine with the Papists, that Christ having freed us, from the eternal punishment, hath not freed us from the temporal. By temporal, we mean the evils both of this life, whether corporeal or spiritual (which are innumerable) and also in the end of this life, viz. an evil death.—Against both these it will be objected, and first against the former; that notwithstanding their justification, the faithful are as subject to afflictions and calamities of this life as others, and therefore to punishment. But I deny that consequence, if you speak of punishments properly, which be the curses of the law afflicted upon men by way of vengeance, to satisfy the justice of God. For the Lord hath imposed the punishment of all our sins upon Christ; who hath fully satisfied the justice of his Father for them. And therefore as there is no condemnation, so no punishment (properly understood) to them that are in Christ Jesus. Neither can it stand with the justice of God (who is not only merciful, but also [l] just in justifying of us) to exact a punishment of the faithful for the satisfying of his justice, for whom Christ hath already fully satisfied his justice by bearing the pu-

k Psalm xci. 10. l Rom. iii. 25, 26; 1 John i. 9.

nishment : this were to punish the same sins twice, once in Christ, and again in us. Indeed the faithful are subject to crosses and afflictions; but all the afflictions of the godly are either trials for their good, or such judgments as are simply fatherly chastisements proceeding from love, and merely respecting the good of the party chastised, whereof the Apostle speaketh, 1 Cor. xi. 32. "[m] When we are judged we are chastised of the Lord, that we should not be condemned with the world," or else they be also τιμωρία (according to the [n] etymology of the word which by some is given) when God besides the chastisement of the party, hath also care to his own honour, which would be impeached, if he should seem to wink at the scandalous offences of his children, as though he would maintain them in their sins. In which regard judgment, as *Peter* [o] saith, beginneth at the house of God. For the Lord many times correcteth those sins in the godly, both for his own honour, and their good, which he seemeth to pass by in the wicked. Of this kind we have an example in *David,* to whom the Lord upon his submission forgave his grievous sins of murder and adultery, notwithstanding both for *David's* chastisement, and for the example of others, but chiefly for the

m 1 Cor. xi. 32. n Of τιμη, honour, and ωρα, care.
o 1 Peter iv. 17.

maintenance of his own glory (which by the scandalous offences of God's children, is by the wicked blasphemed, as though such sins were the fruits of the religion and service of God,) he would not suffer the child begotten in adultery to live. Why? because by that sin *David* had [p] caused the enemies of the Lord to blaspheme. The use which we are to make hereof, is not with the Papists, to teach men to make satisfaction to God for their sins, as though Christ had not fully satisfied for them already: but to teach men, both to beware that they do not commit sin, especially scandalous sins; because thereby they displease and dishonour God their merciful Father, provoking him to pour his judgments upon them, for their amendment, that they be not condemned with the world, and for the maintenance of his own honour: and also that having sinned, we do [q] meet the Lord in his judgments, by humbling ourselves before him, confessing our fault, and craving pardon, that [r] judging ourselves, we may not be judged of the Lord.

Against the second it is also objected, that notwithstanding their justification, the godly die as well as the wicked. I answer, that as of all afflictions, so also of death, the nature is changed in respect of the faithful; to whom death itself, though brought in by the malice

p 2 Sam. xii. 14. q Amos iv. 12. r 1 Cor. xi. 31.

of the devil, is not a curse or punishment properly. I do not deny, but that many times in respect of the time and manner of death, the godly judged and chastised, the Lord in mercy killing their bodies, that he may [s] save their souls; but from the evil of death they are wholly freed, for to them it is the end of sin, and is therefore inflicted upon us, that sin might die with us, as *Methodius* [t] saith, and being the end of sin unto us, it is also the end of misery, the haven of rest, a happy passage out of this vale of misery unto the kingdom of glory; and so not only no curse, but also a blessing, no loss, but an advantage, as after we shall shew. For yet we speak but of the immunities of justification, the principal whereof yet remaineth to be spoken of; that is, freedom from subjection to damnation, to everlasting death, to the eternal wrath of God, which is the most miserable bondage and subjection of all those, who are not justified by faith in Christ. But from this curse also Christ hath freed the faithful. For this is the immunity which we have by him; that "[u] Whosoever believeth in him shall not perish," that there is "[x] no condemnation to them that be in Christ Jesus;" that by his death "[y] he hath destroyed him that had the power of death, that he might

s 1 Cor. xi. 30, 32. t Apud Epiphan. hæres. 64.
u John iii. 16. x Rom. viii 1. y Heb. ii. 15.

deliver them all, which for fear of death, were all their life time subject to bondage;" that Jesus our Saviour delivereth us from the [z] wrath to come.

And thus we have heard of two immunities, which we have in our justification: that we are freed fsom the guilt of sin, and from the curse of the law whereto our sin had made us subject. And from hence ariseth unspeakable peace and liberty to the distressed conscience, terrified with the guilt of sin, the curse of the law, and fear of damnation; when it receiving Christ by faith, hath immunity and freedom from them all.

Sect. 12. *Freedom from the laws exaction of inherent righteousnessto justification.*

Now followeth the other immunity from the law, in respect of the exaction or perfect righteousness to be inherent in us, and perfect obedience to be performed by us, unto our justification and salvation: unto which yoke of bondage, as I said, all men by nature are subject. For it is sure and certain, that without righteousness, and such a righteousness, as is fully answerable to the perfect law of God, no man can be justified.

Now, this righteousness must either be inherent in ourselves, which is the righteousness that the Law requireth unto justification;

z 1 Thes. i. 10.

or being performed by another, (which is Christ) for us, must be imputed unto us : and that is the righteousness which the Gospel propoundeth unto justification.

A third righteousness, whereby we should be justified, cannot be named. If therefore we be not partakers of Christ's righteousness apprehended by faith, we must stand to the sentence of the Law ; which is, either to perform perfect and perpetual obedience, or not to be justified. But if Christ's righteousness be imputed unto us (as it is to all that apprehend it by faith) then are we justified, notwithstanding the sentence of the Law, by [a] faith, (that is, by the righteousness of Christ apprehended by faith) "without the works of the Law," that is, without any respect of obedience performed by ourselves. And in this liberty from the law, standeth the chief comfort and stay of a Christian, when he summoning himself, as it were in the court of his conscience before the judgment seat of God, to be justified, or condemned, shall consider that by Christ he is freed, both from the condemnation of the law, and from the exaction of inherent righteousness to justification : so that he shall not need to stand to the sentence of the Law, or to trust to any obedience performed by himself, as it were to a broken staff, wherein there can be no comfort, (for if

a Rom. iii. 28. Gal. ii. 16.

God should enter into [b] judgment with us according thereto, no man living could be justified) but may safely and freely, without respect, either of his own obedience, or of the sentence of the law, rely upon the mercies of God, and merits of Christ; that for as much as the Lord hath given him grace to believe, and by that faith hath [c] espoused him to Christ, and united him unto him as his member; he hath also communion in Christ's merits, whereby without regard to any righteousness of his own, he is justified before God.

Against this part of Christian liberty, which is most comfortable, the Church of Rome (as it well becomes the synagogue of Antichrist) doth by might and main oppose itself: contending not only that we are justified by righteousness inherent; but also that the same obedience, which the Law prescribeth, is in greater perfection required in the Gospel unto justification. By which doctrine of theirs, they confound the Law and the Gospel, and in so doing abolish the covenant of grace, annihilate the main promise of the Gospel, which is the charter of our liberty, the ground of our faith, the foundation of all our assurance for justification and salvation. For if the Gospel promise and propound justification and salvation, upon the

b Psalm cxliii. 2. c Hos. ii. 20.

condition of our own obedience, and that in more perfection than the law itself required: then is it not only a covenant of works, as well as the law, but also imposeth a heavier yoke upon men's consciences, than the law did. But it is manifest that the Gospel is the covenant of grace made with Abraham[d], concerning justification by faith in Christ; whereas the Law contrarywise is the covenant of works, which four hundred and thirty years after was delivered by Moses, and did not disannul the former promise, concerning justification by faith. The condition whereon the Gospel promiseth justification, is faith in Christ; the condition of the Law, our own perfect and perpetual obedience. For the Gospel[e] saith; if thou believe in Christ, thou art justified and shall be saved: the Law, if thou dost these things, thou shalt live thereby. The righteousness exacted in the Law to justification, is a righteousness both habitual inherent in ourselves, and actually performed by ourselves. The righteousness[f] which without the Law is revealed in the Gospel, is "the Righteousness of God," that is, of Christ who is God, (for he is[g] Jehovah, our righteousness, and was given unto us of God[h] to be our righteousness) "by the faith of Jesus Christ, unto all, and upon all that believe,"

d Gal. iii. 8. 16, 17. e Rom. x. 5, &c.
f Rom. iii. 21, 22. g Jer. xxiii. 6. h 1 Cor. i. 30.

that is, the righteousness of Christ, who is God (though not the righteousness of the Deity, as Osiander thought, but the righteousness both inherent in him, as he was man as his innocency and holiness, and also performed by him, as his passive and active obedience) being apprehended by faith, is according to the doctrine of the Gospel, imputed to every believer unto justification.

That Christ is our righteousness, and "the[i] end of the Law unto righteousness to all that believe, that whosoever[k] believeth in Christ shall be saved," it is the main doctrine of the Gospel, the chief article of our religion, the charter of our inheritance, the assurance which we have of salvation: which we are so to hold, as that if an[l] Angel from Heaven should teach us another Gospel, or propound unto us another way of justification, (as namely by inherent righteousness, and our own obedience) we ought to hold him accursed, and ourselves also, if we yield to him. For whosoever looks to be justified by the obedience which the Law prescribeth, they[m] are separated from Christ, and fallen from grace.

We do not deny, but that the Gospel teacheth repentance as well as faith; and commendeth the duties of sanctification, as

i Rom. x. 4. k John iii. 16. Mark xvi. 16.
l Gal. i. 8, 9. m Gal. v. 4.

well as it promiseth justification. Yea, as it promiseth the grace of justification to those that believe; so to them that are justified and redeemed, it promiseth the[n] grace of sanctification by the spirit, whereby they are enabled in some measure to worship God in holiness and righteousness. We do also confess, that a greater measure of knowledge and obedience is required of the faithful under the Gospel, than was under the Law; because to whom more is given, of them more is required, and the greater benefit requireth the greater duties of thankfulness. But when the question is of the matter of our justification, and merit of our salvation, whereby we being sinners and lost in ourselves, should be justified before God, and entitled unto the kingdom of heaven; what that is, whereby we are absolved from our sins, and accepted as righteous, and as heirs of eternal life; what that is, which will stand in judgment before God, and which we may trust unto, when we appear before the judgment seat of God, why the sentence of condemnation should not be pronounced against us; what that is, whereby we are redeemed from death, and reconciled unto God, or, as the Scripture uttereth the same thing in other terms,[o] whereby we have remission of sins: it is

n Luke i. 74. Jer. xxxi. 33, 34.
o 2 Cor. v. 19. Ephes. i. 7.

most plain, that the doctrine of the Gospel placeth the whole matter of justification, and merit of salvation in the righteousness and obedience of Christ alone; by whose blood, as the Apostle [p] speaketh, and by whose obedience we are justified. As for that righteousness which is inherent in ourselves, though infused of God, and that obedience which is performed by ourselves, though proceeding from grace; the Gospel teacheth us, in the question of justification,[q] to esteem it as dross and dung, yea, as loss, that we may gain Christ, and may be found in him, not having our own righteousness, which is prescribed in the law, but that which is through the law of Christ, the righteousness which is of God through faith.

This therefore is the liberty which we have by the grace of justification, that we are freed from that miserable bondage of the law, which exacteth an obedience and righteousness inherent unto justification, which no man is able to perform, and therefore holdeth men in subjection to damnation, engendering with Agar [r] as the Apostle speaketh, none but servants which shall not inherit with the children of the free woman, that is, who are begotten by the Gospel, to be the heirs of that righteousness which is by faith.

p Rom. v. 9. 18, 19. q Philip. iii. 8, 9.
r Gal. iv. 24, &c.

Sect. 13. *The liberty of justification as it is a right, with the privileges thereof.*

And thus much of the liberty of justification as it is an immunity. For as it is ἐξουσία, or right; it also containeth many notable privileges.

First that we are not only freed from the guilt of sin, but also are accepted, pronounced just, and by imputation of Christ's, both [a] passive and active obedience made righteous, which [b] immediately follows upon the former, so that by our justification we are not only made not guilty, but also stand righteous before God, and that, by the righteousness of Christ.

Secondly, that we are not only freed from the curse of the law, but also are made partakers of the [c] blessedness promised to Abraham, viz. that in his [d] seed, which is Christ, the faithful of all nations should be blessed. But this will best appear in the particulars: for the faithful are not only freed from the evils of this life, whether corporeal or spiritual, as they be curses; but they are all turned into blessings unto them. For this is the privilege of the faithful, that the Lord causeth all things, whether good or bad,[e] "To work together for the good of those that do love him." In which sense David saith,[f] that "all things

a Rom. v. 9. 19. b Rom. iv. 6, 7; 2 Cor. v. 21.
c Gal. iii. 13, 14. 16. d Gen. xxii. 18.
e Rom. viii. 28. f Psal. i. 3.

succeed well with the righteous man." As for afflictions, he both professeth in particular of himself,[g] that "it was good for him that he had been afflicted;" and also in general pronounceth the man[h] "blessed, whom the Lord doth chastise and teach in his law."

Again, corporeal death is not only no loss to the faithful; but also an advantage; because in it they change a sinful and mortal life, for a life blessed and immortal. It is not only no curse, but also a blessing: for it is not only the end of sin and misery, but the beginning of perfect and everlasting happiness: whereupon the Holy Ghost[i] pronounceth them all "blessed that die in the Lord."

Neither are the faithful only freed from fear of damnation, but also are put in assurance of everlasting life, being[k] saved in hope, which is the chief happiness that can be enjoyed in this life.

Thirdly, we are not only freed from the sentence of the law, exacting of us perfect obedience unto justification, but we have also liberty to plead the righteousness propounded in the covenant of grace; and to appeal from the sentence of the law, to the promise of the Gospel; from the tribunal of justice to the throne of grace; and in the

g Psal. cxix. 71. h Psal. xciv. 12, 13.
i Apoc. xiv. 13. k Rom. viii. 24.

question of justification not at all to regard our own obedience, but wholly to rest upon the mercies of God, and merits of Christ our Saviour.

Upon this liberty of justification follow other privileges. For first, whereas by nature we are the children of wrath; now,[l] "being justified by faith, we have peace with God, through our Lord Jesus Christ, who hath [m] reconciled us to himself.

2. Whereas sin maketh a [n] separation between God and us, so that naturally we shun the presence of God, as of a severe Judge; being justified by the righteousness of Christ, we also have free [o] access unto God by faith, and have liberty with boldness and assurance that we shall be heard, to make our requests to God in the name of Christ.

3. Upon our justification by faith, we are endued with the spirit of adoption,[p] which assureth us of God's fatherly love towards us, teaching us to cry in our hearts, *Abba, Father;* by which, being the earnest of our inheritance, we are sealed up unto the day of our full redemption.

4. With the hope of salvation, which is [q] a companion of justifying faith, and a conse-

l Rom. v. 1. m Colos. i. 20, 21. n Isa. lix. 2.
o Rom. v. 2; Ephes. iii. 12; 1 John v. 14.
p Rom. v. 5; Ephes. i. 13; Rom. viii. 15, 16; Gal. iv. 6; Ephes. iv. 30. q Rom. viii. 23; Tit. ii. 13.

quent of justification, whereby we live in expectation of everlasting happiness.

5. With joy[r] in the Holy Ghost, which Peter calleth joy unspeakable and glorious. For the Apostle denying that the liberty of Christians doth chiefly stand in[s] meat and drink, and in the free use of outward things; sheweth also wherein it principally doth consist. For " the kingdom of God (saith he) is not meat and drink, but righteousness," which is the privilege of justification itself, " and peace and joy in the Holy Ghost," which are consequences of the former.

Lastly, with perseverance. For[t] as the Son abideth in the house for ever, being[u] safely kept by the power of God through faith unto salvation. For if [x] sons, then heirs, heirs of God, and coheirs with Christ, &c.

Sect. 14. The liberty of sanctification. 1. From the dominion of sin.

Now I come to the liberty which we have in our sanctification, and so far forth as we are sanctified. Now our sanctification in this life being but in part, so is this liberty: which, as it is an immunity, is also a freedom from the bondage of sin, and of the law; though in other re-

r Rom. v. 2, 3; 1 Pet. i. 8. s Rom. xiv. 17.
t John viii. 35. u 1 Pet. i. 5, φρουρȣμενȣς.
x Rom. viii. 17.

spects, then those that have been mentioned in the liberty of justification.

For, in justification we are freed from the guilt of sin, in sanctification, from the corruption of sin. But here we are to consider, how far forth we are set free therefrom. For the hypocritical Papists teach, that when a man is regenerated, or as they also speak, justified, original sin is so abolished, as that it doth not only not reign, but not so much as remain or live in the party sanctified. By which doctrine they teach men to be desperate hypocrites, either searing their conscience, that they may have no sense of sin, and may please themselves with this conceit, that they have no sin; in which respect the saying of Peter [a] is verified of them, that while they promise liberty to themselves and others, they are indeed servants of corruption: or if they have any sense of sin dwelling in them, they must persuade themselves they are not sanctified, nor justified, and therefore not to be saved: such miserable comforters they are of poor sinners, as to persuade them that they have not remission of sin, until sin be quite abolished in them. But this doctrine they teach contrary to the evident testimonies of Scripture, contrary to the perpetual experience of the faithful, contrary

a 2 Pet. ii. 19.

to the light of their own conscience; that they might thereby uphold their Antichristian doctrine of justification by inherent righteousness, and of the merit of good works, which otherwise would fall to the ground. For, if in respect of original sin, remaining and dwelling in us, we be in ourselves sinners: how can we be justified by inherent righteousness? If our best actions be stained with the flesh, how should they merit eternal life?

We are therefore to hold, that in regeneration we are freed from the corruption of sin; not wholly, and at once, but in part, and by degrees; that sin (though mortified in part, and we freed from the tyranny of it, that it reign no more with full swing and authority in us) still remaineth and dwelleth in us, hindering us from good, provoking us unto evil, defiling and contaminating our best actions, never suffering us with the full consent of[b] will, to perform or desire that which is good. As the Apostle plainly sheweth by his own example, Rom. vii.[c] where the concupiscence remaining in him, is not only plainly called a sin, but described as a sin, and as an *ἀνομία*, or a repugnancy to the law of God: the sense whereof (though the Papists have no sense of it) made the holy Apostle cry out,

b Gal. v. 17. c Rom. vii. 14, &c.

[d] "Miserable man that I am, who shall deliver me from this body of death?" Accursed, therefore, was the council of Trent,[e] which, confessing that the Apostle calleth it a sin; notwithstanding pronounceth them accursed, that shall say it is a sin. But, if we say we have no sin, we deceive ourselves, saith St. John,[f] and there is no truth in us.

The freedom, therefore, which we have in our sanctification, which as Augustine saith, is but begun in this life, is not from the being of sin in us altogether and at once, though we be freed from it, in part and by degrees, but from the dominion of it, that we should no more be servants of sin, but being freed from sin, might become servants of righteousness, Rom. vi. 6. 18, which Augustine[g] did well observe out of the words of the Apostle, dehorting us that sin should not remain in our mortal bodies. "He doth not say, let it not be; but, let it not reign: for while thou livest, it cannot be avoided, but that sin will be in thy members; nevertheless let dominion be taken from it," &c. Of this liberty the Apostle speaketh, Rom. viii. [h] the "law of the spirit of life which is in Christ, hath made me free from the law of sin and of death."

d Rom. vii. 24. e Sess. v. f 1 John i. 8.
g In John, tract. 41. h Rom. viii. 2.

That is, the power of the quickening Spirit, which being in Christ our head, and from him communicated unto us, doth rule in us as a law, doth free us from the power of sin which worketh death, that it no more have dominion (as it were a law) in us. And Rom. vi.[i] having proved, that sin neither doth, nor can any more reign in the faithful, because after the similitude of Christ's death and resurrection, they are dead to sin and risen again; and therefore, as death can no more have dominion over Christ, being risen from death, no more can sin have dominion over the faithful being once risen from the grave of sin: afterwards, verse 14, he assureth the faithful, that sin shall[k] not have dominion over them, because they be not under the law, but under grace. Likewise St. John[l] saith, "He that is born of God, doth not commit sin," namely, as a servant of sin: yea, he addeth, that "he cannot sin," namely, with full swing and consent of will, as those which be servants of sin; because the seed of God remaineth in him, whereby he is partly spirit, and not only flesh. And, therefore, as he cannot perfectly will that which is good, because of the reluctation of the flesh; so can he not will with full consent, that which is evil, because of the reluctation of the spirit.

i Rom. vi. 2, &c. ad 12. k Rom. vi. 14.
l 1 John iii. 9; John viii. 34.

Sect. 15. *2. Freedom from the dominion of the law.*

Secondly, we are in our sanctification freed from the law. But we are here also to consider, *quatenus*, how far forth. For the [a]Papists charge us, that we place Christian liberty in this, that we are subject to no law in our conscience, and before God; and that we are free from all necessity of doing good works: which is a most devilish slander. For although they absurdly confound justification and sanctification; yet they know we do not: neither are they ignorant, but that we put a great difference between them in this respect. For though we teach that the obedience of the law is not required in us to justification, but that we are freed from the exaction of the law in that behalf: yet we deny not, but that unto sanctification on the obedience of the law is required, and we by necessity of duty, bound to the observation thereof. We confess that to be free from obedience, is to be the servants of sin, and the willing and cheerful worship of God, [b]in holiness and righteousness without fear, to be true liberty. We acknowledge that the moral law of God is perpetual, immutable; and that this is an everlasting truth, that the creature is bound to worship and obey his Creator, and so much the more bound, as he hath received greater benefits.

a Bellarm. de justif. lib. iv. cap. 5 and c. 1.
b Luke. xvii. 4.

Indeed we say with *Luther*,[c] that in our justification we are restored to a state of justice, from which *Adam* fell; but yet, as we teach that we are no more bound to obedience, that thereby we might be justified, than *Adam* who was already just; so we profess, that in allegiance and thankfulness, we are more bound to obey than he, yea, we profess that God doth therefore free us from the curse, and the bondage of the law, that we might be enabled with freedom of spirit to obey it; and that being freed from sin,[d] we are made the servants of righteousness. We teach, that God having sworn[e], that to those whom he justifieth, he will give grace to worship him in holiness and righteousness; no man can be assured of his justification without obedience: that sanctification being the end of our [f] election, calling, redemption, and regeneration, it is a necessary consequent of saving grace. We teach and profess, that howsoever good works do not concur with faith, unto the act of justification, as a cause thereof; yet they concur in the party justified, as necessary fruits of faith, and testimonies of justification. And as we teach with *Paul*[g], that faith alone doth justify; so with *James*[h], that the faith which is alone doth not justify. We teach, that the blood

c De libert. Christ. d Rom. vi. 18. e Luke i. 73, 74.
f Ephes. i. 4; 1 Thes. iv. 7. Titus ii. 14.; Ephes. ii. 10.
g Rom. iii. 28; Gal. ii. 16. h James ii. 14, &c.

of Christ, as it acquitteth us from the guilt of sin; so doth it also purge[i] our consciences from dead works, to serve the living God; that "he bare[k] in his body upon the cross our sins, that we being delivered from sin, should live in righteousness:" that whom Christ doth justify by faith, them he doth sanctify by his Spirit; that "Whosoever[l] is in Christ he is a new creature,"[m] crucifying the flesh with the lusts thereof, and[n] walking not after the flesh, but after the spirit. We profess that good works are necessary to salvation, though not *necessitate efficientiæ*, as causing it as the Papists teach; yet *necessitate præsentiæ*, as necessary fruits of our faith, whereby we are to glorify God, and to testify our thankfulness, to do good to our brethren, and to make sure[o] our election, calling and justification unto ourselves; as necessary forerunners of salvation, being the undoubted badges of them that shall be saved, being the way wherein we are to[p] walk to everlasting life, being the evidence according to which God will judge us at the last day. And lastly, that as by justification God doth entitle us unto his kingdom; so by sanctification he doth fit and prepare us thereto.

We do not therefore by the doctrine of justification through faith, abolish the law,

i Heb. ix. 14. k 1 Peter ii. 24. l 2 Cor. v. 17.
m Gal. v. 24. n Rom. viii. 1. o 2 Pet. i. 10.
p Eph. ii. 10.

but rather as the Apostle saith,[q] stablish it. For the more a man is assured of his free justification, the better he is enabled, and the more he is bound to obey it.

But although we be bound to obey the law, as the subjects of God, and servants of righteousness; and although the law hath singular use in those that are justified, (as being a rule of direction for our obedience, in the performance of the duties of piety towards God, of justice towards our neighbour, of sobriety towards ourselves; and a glass of detection, to manifest the imperfections of our obedience, to keep us from Pharisaism: and lastly, a rod of correction, in respect of flesh or the old man yet remaining in us, that by precepts, by exhortations and comminations, it more and more may be mortified in us, and we keep from the spirit of slumber and security:) yet notwithstanding we are "not under the law," as the[r] Apostle saith, "but under grace." We are therefore in our sanctification freed, though not from the obedience, yet from the servitude and bondage of the law, and that in three respects:

Sect. 16. *Freedom from the irritation of the law.*

First, in respect of the irritation of it. In which regard especially the law is called the[a] strength of sin: not that the

q Rom. iii. 31. r Rom. vi. 14. a 1 Cor. xv. 56.

law causeth or provoketh sin properly, for the [b] law is holy, just and good; but only by accident, and occasionally. For such is the corruption of our untamed nature until we be [c] renewed by the Spirit of God; that when the law, which is holy and good, forbiddeth sin, seeking to stop the course of our concupiscences, and to bridle our sinful affections; thereby our untamed corruption rebelleth so much the more; and that it might appear [d] *καθ' ὑπερβολην ἁμαρτωλὸς*, exceedingly sinful, by occasion of the law worketh in us all manner of concupiscence. Even, as a deep river, when nothing hindereth his course, hath a still, and as it were a dead motion; but if you seek to restrain or stop his course, he will swell and overflow all, now disdaining, as it were, a bridge: so our corruption, when it freely taketh his own course, seemeth to be quiet, and as it were dead: but when the commandment cometh,[e] saith the Apostle, as it were to dam it up, sin reigneth and riseth against it, swelling and overfloweth as it were, his wonted banks. In this respect, the law (saith the Master of the [f] Sentences) 'is called a killing letter,

b Rom. vii. 12.

c Nitimur in vetitum semper cupimusq. negata. Gens humana ruit in vetitum nefas. quod non licet, acrius urit.

d Rom. vii. 13. 8. e Rom. vii. 9.

f Lib. iii. dict. 40. B.

because forbidding sin, it increaseth concupiscence, and addeth transgression until grace do free us." But we are regenerated by the spirit of sanctification, and by the bond of the same spirit coupled unto Christ; we are freed from this bondage even as the wife is freed from the dominion of her husband by his death. For even as whilst we were in the flesh altogether unregenerate, the law, as it were our husband, occasionally and by accident begot in our souls, wholly corrupted with sin, evil motions and concupiscences, as the fruits and issue of our flesh tending unto death; so we being regenerated, and after a sort dead unto this corruption, and consequently being mortified to the law in respect of the irritation thereof, and the law in that regard dead unto us, the Spirit of Christ, who hath united us unto him as our second husband, begetteth good motions in us as the fruits of the spirit, acceptable unto God. This is that which the Apostle teacheth,[g] Rom. vii. for having said, chap. vi. 14, that sin shall not have dominion over us, because we are not under the law but under grace, after he had answered an objection, and prevented the abuse of this doctrine which carnal men would make thereof, as though they might sin freely, because they are not under the law: in the beginning of the seventh chapter he proveth that we are not under the

g Rom. vii. 1, &c.

law, but under grace, by that similitude which even now I mentioned: because being regenerated and dead unto sin, we are mortified to the law, and the law to us in respect of the irritation thereof, caused by our corruption, and consequently are delivered from the power of it, as a wife is freed from the dominion of her husband when he is dead.

Freedom from terror or coaction of the law.

Secondly, in our sanctification we are freed from the coaction and terror of the law, breeding servile fear in men unregenerate, whereby, as bond-servants or galley-slaves, by the whip they are enforced to the performance of some outward duties, which otherwise they are unwilling to do. For those who are under the law, as all men are by nature, are like bond-slaves, who, for avoiding of punishment, are by terror drawn to do some forced service, which is so much the more unwilling, because they look for no reward. This, in the Scripture, is called sometimes *πνεῦμα δȣλείας*, [h] "the spirit of bondage," and sometimes *πνεῦμα δειλείας*,[i] "the spirit of fear," from which we are delivered when we receive the spirit of adoption and sanctification, whereby we are enabled to worship God in holiness and righteousness, *ἀφόβως*, without servile fear, according to the covenant of grace made with Abraham,

h Rom. viii. 15. i 2 Tim. i. 7.

Luke i.[k] And in this sense it is said, that the law[l] is not imposed on the just, to whom, being as it were a law unto themselves, and willingly performing that which is right, the terror and coaction of the law, so far forth as they are regenerate, is needless.

Freedom from the rigour or exaction of the law.

Thirdly, as we are freed from the coaction and terror of the law, so also from the exaction and rigour of the law, which they call *τὸ ἀκριβοδίκαιον*, which though it be a liberty of sanctification, and appertaining to our new obedience; yet it dependeth on the liberty of justification. For as there we were freed from the law's exaction of inherent righteousness, to the acceptation of our persons; so here we are freed from the law's exaction of perfect obedience to the acceptation of our actions. So that whereas the law condemneth every the least imperfection or defect, not agreeing with that perfection of justice, which it prescribeth, as a sin, or *ἀνομία*, and pronounceth the party in whom that defect or imperfection is, accursed; notwithstanding the new obedience of God's children, wrought in them by the Spirit of God, and performed according to the measure of grace received, though defective in itself, and stained with the flesh, is accepted of God; who covereth their imperfection, with the perfect obedience of Christ, and not so much respecteth the

k Luke i. 74. l 1 Tim. i. 9.

perfection of the outward act, which he doth not expect from such weakness, as the integrity of the heart, the uprightness of the will and desire, the sincerity of the endeavour; which if it be not wanting, the Lord[m] accepteth the will for the deed, and true endeavour striving[n] towards perfection for the perfect performance. In which respect the Lord according to his gracious promise,[o] useth clemency towards us as a tender father useth clemency towards his son, taking in good part the childish endeavour of his children, proceeding from an unfeigned desire to please him.*

Sect. 17. *The liberty of sanctification as it is a right, with the privileges thereof.*

But our liberty in sanctification is not only an immunity, but also an *ἐξουσία*, or right, consisting of great privileges. For, first we are not only freed in part from the corruption of sin, which we call mortification; but are also positively made righteous, being, as the Apostle Peter speaketh, made partakers[a] of the Divine nature, in that flying from the corruption which is in the world by lust, we are renewed according to the[b] image of God, in holiness

m 2 Cor. viii. 12. n Phil. iii. 14, 15.
o Mal. iii. 17. Psalm ciii. 13.

* The sentiment here expressed, must be carefully distinguished from the erroneous doctrine of justification by a modified law. The author is speaking of the *actions of a justified person, not of the actions whereby a person is justified.*—Ed.

a 2 Pet. i. 4. b Eph. i. 24.

and righteousness. For as the sacred oil being poured on the head of[c] Aaron (who was a type of Christ) distilled unto his lower parts: so the[d] oil of grace wherewith Christ our head was anointed[e] without measure, is derived even to his inferior members here on earth, who are also therewith[f] anointed,[g] receiving of his fulness, even grace for grace. Neither are we only freed from the servitude of sin, satan, and the world, but in Christ our king, who hath overcome[h] the world, and triumphed over sin and satan, we are also made kings,[i] with assurance to be conquerors of all the enemies of our salvation.

And as touching the Law, we are not only freed from the irritation thereof, whereunto our own corruption did make us subject, as unto a husband, who begot foul issue of us tending to death, and so left at large: but we are also joined to another husband which is Christ, by his Spirit, whereby[k] he produceth in us the fruits of the spirit, to the glory of God. Neither doth the law only cease to provoke us unto sin; but when we are once sanctified, it becometh, as David[l] speaketh, a counsellor unto us, and a director unto good things.

c Psalm cxxxiii. d Psalm xlv. 8. e John iii. 34.
f 2 Cor. i. 21. 1 John ii. 20, 27. g John i. 16.
h John xvi. 33. Col. ii. 15. i Apocal. i. 6.
Rom. xvi. 20. 2 Cor. ii. 14. Rom viii. 37.
k Rom. vii. 4. l Psalm cxix. 24.

Neither are we freed only from the spirit of bondage and fear, but are also indued with the spirit of liberty and grace, the spirit [m] of adoption, the spirit of [n] power and of love, and of sobriety: which spirit having shed [o] abroad the love of God in our hearts, testifying unto us our adoption, and as an [p] earnest assuring us of our inheritance, and enflaming our hearts with a reciprocal love of God, and of our neighbour for his sake: we begin to delight [q] in the law of God, as concerning the inner man, neither are the commandments of God [r] grievous unto us, and we begin to serve the Lord not only without fear, but also with [s] willing minds and upright hearts. For those who are redeemed and sanctified by Christ, are עם נדבות,[t] "a people of willingness,"[u] a people peculiar to himself, zealous of good works.

And lastly, concerning the rigour of the Law; we have not only this immunity, that the imperfections of our sincere obedience are not imputed to us; but also this privilege, that our imperfect obedience, which in itself is worthy to be rejected, notwithstanding is both accepted of God, and rewarded. For Christ having washed us with his blood, and sanctified us by his spirit, hath made us both

m Rom. viii. 15. n 2 Tim. i. 7. o Rom. v. 5.
p Ephes. i. 14. q Rom. vii. 22. Ps. i. 2, cxix. 24.
r 1 John v. 3. s 1 Chron. xxviii. 9. t Ps. cx. 3.
u Titus ii. 14.

kings, as I said before, and also [x] Priests, or as Peter speaketh [y], "a royal and holy priesthood, to offer spiritual sacrifices acceptable to God by Jesus Christ:" the sacrifice of obedience whereby we offer ourselves [z] "as a lively, holy, and acceptable sacrifice unto God, which is our reasonable service:" the sacrifice of alms, whereby we offer our goods, with which [a] "sacrifices God is well pleased:" the sacrifice of a broken and contrite heart [b], which is to God instead of all sacrifices: the sacrifice of prayer, which is accepted [c] as incense, and as the evening sacrifice: the sacrifice of praise, that is, the [d] fruit, or as Hosea [e] speaketh, the calves of our lips, which the Lord preferreth [f] before the sacrifices of goats and bulls: all which, though in themselves defective and imperfect, are notwithstanding acceptable unto God, through the mediation of Christ; who, making intercession for us, perfumeth [g] all these sacrifices of ours, with the odours of his own sacrifice, that so they may be acceptable, and sweet smelling savours unto God.

Neither are they only accepted, but also rewarded. For our [h] obedience, our [i] confidence, our patience, our [k] prayer, fasting,

x Apocal. i. 6. y 1 Pet. ii. 5, 9. z Rom. xii. 1.
a Heb. xiii. 16. b Ps. li. 19. c Ps. cxli. 2.
d Heb. xiii. 15. e Hos. xiv. 3. f Ps. l. 13, 14, 23.
g Apoc. viii. 3, 4. h Prov. xi. 18. Ps. xix. 11.
i Heb. x. 35. Jas. i. 12. k Matt. vi. 4, 6, 18.

alms, and[l] charitable deeds have their rewards, in so much that[m] a cup of cold water given in charity, shall not lose his reward. In respect whereof, we may well say with "David,[n] unto thee Lord, mercy: for thou rewardest a man according to his works." Which plainly proveth, that the reward of our obedience is not to be ascribed to the merit of our works, (which in themselves cannot stand in judgment) but to the mercies of God in Christ. For there is greater mercy in not imputing unto us the imperfections of our works; greater in accepting of them as if they were perfect; but greatest of all in rewarding them. The consideration whereof, ought to animate and stir us up with willing and cheerful minds, to obey God, to serve him, to call upon him, and to perform such duties as he requireth of us; because we are to be assured, that he doth not impute unto us our wants, but accept our imperfect obedience, and not only favourably accept it, but also graciously reward it.

Sect. 18. *The special liberty of Christians, or that which is peculiar to the faithful under the Gospel.*

Hitherto we have spoken of the common liberty of Christians: which being (as we have heard) conferred upon us in our vocation, justification, and sanctification; we are to be exhorted to give all diligence, both that we

l Luke vi. 35. m Matt. x. 42. n Ps. lxii. 13.

may be called, justified, and sanctified, and that our calling, justification, and sanctification may be made sure unto us, by leading a godly life. For if we be not sanctified, nor justified, nor called, then are we (whatsoever we are, rich or poor, noble or base, learned or unlearned) the most miserable bond-slaves of sin and satan ; and being servants, howsoever for a time we retain a place in the house of God, yet we shall not abide for ever, but when the time of separation cometh, we shall be cast out: whereas contrarywise being made free by our calling, justification, sanctification, as the sons of God, we shall have the privilege of sons, which is,[a] to abide in the house of God for ever.

Now followeth the Christian liberty, which is peculiar to the faithful under the Gospel. For the faithful under the old Testament, though they were sons and heirs, and therefore enjoyed the former liberties by Christ, in whom they believed, notwithstanding until the fulness of time came, which was the full age of the Church, they were under years; and therefore as sons during their minority, were subject to[b] schoolmasters and tutors, whereby are meant the pedagogy and government of the typical Church of the Jews, contained in the ceremonial and judicial laws of Moses; in which regard they, though sons,

a John viii. 35. b Gal. iv. 1, &c. and iii. 24.

seemed little to differ from servants. Both these laws were appendices of the law moral: the ceremonial, of the first table, determining the particulars of that peculiar worship which he prescribed to the typical Church, until the coming of Christ. The judicial, of the second, determining the particulars of the peculiar policy which he prescribed to the commonwealth of the Jews. So that the ceremonial, were the ecclesiastical laws of that Church; the judicial, the civil laws of that commonwealth. Both were yokes of bondage, as the Apostle speaketh [c], in respect of the Jews, on whose consciences these laws were imposed, binding them to the strict observation thereof; in regard whereof, they are called an [d] unsupportable yoke, under which notwithstanding, the faithful were *δέδȣλωμένοι*, [e] held in bondage. And as touching the Gentiles, they were as a [f] wall of separation between them and the Jews, and as the door of Noah's Ark, excluding all from salvation that were not of that Church, either as born Jews, or as proselytes. For the rest "were without [g] Christ, aliens from the Commonwealth of Israel, strangers from the covenants of promise, having no hope, living without God in the world." This wall of partition [h] our Saviour Christ by his

c Gal. v. 1. d Acts xv. 10. e Gal. iv. 3.
f Eph. ii. 14. g Eph. ii. 12. h Eph. ii. 14. &c.

death hath dissolved, taking away all difference[i] between Jews and Gentiles, freeing and exempting both the one and the other, from the obedience both of the judicial and ceremonial law, which were given to put a difference between the Jews and the Gentiles, until the fulness of time,[k] Gal. iv. 4. the time [l] of reformation, that is, until the coming of the Messiah, by whose death they were to be [m] abrogated. For howsoever the faithful, before the Church came to full age, were in bondage under the ceremonial, and judicial law, as under schoolmasters and tutors; yet,[n] when "the fulness of time came, God sent his Son born of a woman, and born under the law, that he might redeem them that were under the law:" meaning that we are redeemed, not only from the moral law, in the respects before named; but also from the ceremonial and judicial, even in respect of obedience.

For as touching the ceremonial law, as it was an [o] hand-writing of ordinances which was (though underhand) against us; Christ hath cancelled it, and nailed it to his cross. As it was a [p] shadow and figure of things to come, Christ hath abolished it, by performing that indeed, which it did but shadow and

i Acts xv. 9. k Gal. iv. 4. l Heb. ix. 10.
m 2 Cor. iii. 11, 13. n Gal. iv. 3, 4, 5.
o Col. ii. 14. ὑπεναντίον. Eph. ii 15.
p Heb. x. 1. Col. ii. 17. John i. 17.

prefigure: for the law was given by Moses; but grace and truth by Christ. For as grace is opposed to the curse, so truth to figures: the ceremonies therefore of the law gave place as shadows to the body, and as figures to the truth.

The civil or judicial law, being the positive laws of that people, Christ abrogated, when according to the prophecy of Daniel,[q] he destroying the Commonwealth of the Jews, their city and temple, did with all abolish their policy and laws. For the very city, temple, and whole state of the Jews, being types and shadows of Christ and his Church, were, when Christ was exhibited, and his universal Church by preaching the Gospel to all nations, planted[r], to give place; and with them, their laws; which were to hold but till the fulness of time. For as the Apostle saith, the Priesthood (namely, of Aaron) being translated[s], the law (namely of Moses) is also translated.

Howbeit there is some difference between the abrogating of the ceremonial, and of the judicial law: the ceremonial rites, because they were principally ordained to prefigure Christ, are so abolished, that it is not lawful for Christians to observe them, for that were to deny that Christ is come. *Ea non obser-*

q Dan. ix. 26, 27. r Matt. xxiv. 14.
s 2 Heb. vii. ii.

vant Christiani (saith[t] Augustine) *per quæ Christus promittebatur; nec adhuc promittuntur, quia jam impleta sunt:* "Christians do not observe those things, by which Christ was promised; neither are they still promised, because they are already fulfilled." The judicial ordinances, because they principally tended to the observation of justice and equity, may be used, so they be not imposed or observed by virtue of the judicial law: for that were, though indirectly, to deny that the Messiah is already come. Both laws were dead with Christ, though they were not buried, but as it were, kept above ground, even by Christians among the Jews, until the dissolution of the temple and city of Jerusalem. After which time, the ceremonial precepts were not only dead, as[u] one saith, but also deadly to the observers of them, but the judicials not so.

Sect. 19. *Peculiar Christian liberty, as it is an immunity.*

Now, this Christian liberty as it is an immunity, is a freedom from all bond of conscience, in respect of outward things, which are neither commanded nor forbidden in the eternal law of God. Of which there are two sorts, the ordinances of men concerning things indifferent, and the creatures of God.

t Contra faustum Minich. lib. 19. cap. 18.
u Tho. 1. 2. quest. 104.

For as touching the former, seeing there is no law that bindeth the conscience properly, but only the law of God, in which sense he is called[a] our only Law-giver, and seeing we are freed from those laws of God, which determined those particulars, which are neither commanded nor forbidden in the moral law of God: it is plain, therefore, that our conscience is free in respect of these things. As for the laws of men, whether they be ecclesiastical or civil, they do not properly bind the conscience; because neither is simple obedience due unto them, neither can they make any particular, which in respect of the moral law, is indifferent, as being neither commanded nor forbidden, to be simply necessary. The conscience of a Christian is exempted from human power, and cannot be bound, but where God doth bind it. And therefore the Apostle, as he chargeth the Corinthians, that, seeing they were[b] bought with a price, they should not be the servants of men, (which is not to be understood of external servitude, but of the bondage of the conscience) and likewise the Colossians,[c] that "no man should condemn them," (that is, take upon him to bind the conscience with guilt of sin) "in respect of meat and drink, or holy days:" so he reproveth the[d] Colossians, for ob-

a James iv. 12. b 1 Cor. vii. 23.
c Col. ii. 16. d Col. ii. 20, 21, 22.

serving the traditions of men, with opinion of necessity, as if the conscience were bound by them, or religion were to be placed in them.

Herein therefore the Church of Rome is also an enemy to Christian liberty, not only in burthening Christians with an heap of innumerable traditions and ceremonies; but chiefly, in imposing them upon the conscience: teaching, that the traditions of the church are with like [e] reverence, and equal affection of piety to be received, as the written word of God; and that the commandments of the church, even concerning outward things, do bind the conscience, and although many of their ceremonies be wicked; more, ridiculous; most of them, superfluous; yet so absurd they are, as to impose them to be observed, not only with opinion of necessity, as binding the conscience, but also of worship, of perfection, of merit, of spiritual efficacy.

Secondly, by this liberty we are freed from scrupulosity of conscience, in respect of the creatures, which are ordained for our use; the difference of clean and unclean (which was made by the ceremonial law) being taken away. "Nothing," saith our Saviour Christ,[f] "that goeth into the mouth,

e Conc. Trid. Sess. 4.
f Matt. xv. 11.

defileth a man." And Paul,[g] "I know," saith he, "and am persuaded by the Lord Jesus, that there is nothing common or unclean of itself."

Sect. 20. Peculiar Christian liberty, as it is a right.

But this liberty is not only an immunity, but also an ἐξουσία or power, both in respect of the ordinances of men, and also of the creatures of God. For, being freed from the ceremonial, and judicial laws of God, and therefore not tied to any particular or certain laws, which should determine the particulars not mentioned in the word of God: hereupon ariseth a liberty, both to law-givers, and those who are subject to laws. The law-givers are not restrained to any particulars, but have liberty to ordain such wholesome, either constitutions ecclesiastical, or laws civil, as are not repugnant to the word of God. Laws there must be, to determine the particulars not mentioned in the general law of God; for they are the very bond of human societies, necessary for the execution of the laws of God, and for the maintenance of peace and order among men. Neither can it be denied, but that as the judicial law being abolished, it is lawful for law-givers to ordain civil laws; so likewise the ceremonial law being

g Rom. xiv. 14.

abrogated, to establish laws ecclesiastical. Only the question is, who must be these law-givers. Surely, not the Presbyteries of every parish, which never were in use in the primitive church, but Synods; as appeareth by the perpetual practice of the church, both in the Apostles' times, and ever since. Synods, I say, either provincial, or national; and those assembled, either out of some nation, or out of some more than one, which some call *consilia media*, or lastly general. The authority of Synods provincial and national hath always been of great regard, though there want a Christian Magistrate to second and confirm them, being both assembled and moderated by the authority of Metropolitans and Archbishops; but when both national Synods are assembled, and the Synodal constitutions ratified by the authority of the Sovereign, and that according to the positive laws of the land, authorizing him so to do; I see not, why men should not as well think themselves bound to observe laws ecclesiastical, as civil. For though some make a difference between them in this behalf, because civil laws determining particulars belonging to the second table, cannot be violated without breaking the second table, whereas ecclesiastical laws determining particulars appertaining to the first table, may be broken without transgressing of the first table; yet, who seeth not the weakness of this distinction: seeing the second table is broken by disobeying the lawful authority of superiors (which we ought to obey for conscience sake) as well by transgressing the one, as the other. Superiors in the church are to be honoured and obeyed by the fifth commandment, and other Scriptures,[a] as well as superiors, in the commonwealth. And if their constitutions, when they wanted the concurrence of a Christian magistrate, were of force in the primitive church; then much greater is their validity, being confirmed by the authority of the Sovereign, and the Sovereign authorized thereunto by law.

The freedom of the subject is, that being freed from the yoke of the judicial and ceremonial law, he may with a free conscience obey any other laws, whether ecclesiastical or civil, which being not dissonant from the word of God, are or shall be imposed upon him. Which, though it be a plain and evident truth, yet by some men it is not observed.

And as touching the use of the creatures, and of all things indifferent, we are to know, that the right and dominion we had over the creatures, which was lost in Adam, is restored in Christ, (for all are yours, saith the Apostle,[b] and you are Christ's,) and that

a Heb. xiii. 17. b 1 Cor. iii. 22.

not only for Christians under the Gospel, but also for all the faithful from the beginning. For we read, Gen. ix.,[c] that to Noah, who was the heir[d] of the righteousness, which is by faith, the grant was renewed, and free use of the creatures permitted. Howbeit this freedom was by the ceremonial law restrained, not only after the giving of the law of Moses; but also before, a difference being put[e] between things clean and unclean: which difference by Christ is taken away. For, no[f] creature is unclean of itself, but every[g] creature is good, and nothing to be refused, but may be received with thanksgiving. Yea, of all outward things, not forbidden of God, which commonly are called things indifferent, the Apostle affirmeth in general, that[h] "all things are lawful," and[i] "to the pure all things are pure." By this liberty therefore the faithful are privileged, with freedom of conscience, to use or forbear any of the creatures of God created for our use, or things indifferent, without opinion of necessity to be brought[k] under the power thereof, or placing religion therein. In which respect, Basil fitly calleth things indifferent, *τὰ ἐν ἐξȣσία*, things in our power or left to our liberty.

c Gen. ix. 2, 3. d Heb. xi. 7. e Gen. vii. 2; ix. 4. f Rom. xiv. 14. g 1 Tim. iv. 4. h 1 Cor. vi. 12. i Tit. i. 15. k 1 Cor. vi. 11.

Sect. 21. Application of the general doctrine to this particular.

1. That this also is a liberty of the sons of God.

But here for avoiding of error, three things are from the general doctrine to be repeated. First, that this also is a liberty of the sons of God: secondly, that it is spiritual: and thirdly, that it is a true liberty. For as touching the first, though all things be pure to the pure; yet [a] "to them that are unclean and unbelieving, nothing is clean." Though to [b] the faithful all these outward things are lawful; yet to the wicked and unbelievers nothing is lawful, yea, those actions, which are materially good as being commanded of God, as they proceed from them, are turned into sin. Which is spoken, not to this end, to drive me into desperate courses; but to force them, without farther delays, to break off the course of their sins by speedy and unfeigned repentance, and to sue unto God for mercy and pardon in Christ; because this is the only thing which they may lawfully do and without sin, and which until they do, they do nothing else but sin, and by sin hoard up wrath against the day of wrath, &c.

2. That this also is a spiritual liberty.

Secondly, though this liberty concerns outward things; yet itself is inward and spiritual, as being a liberty of the conscience. Now the

a Tit. i. 15. b Cor. vi. 12.; 1 Tim. iv. 3.

conscience respecteth God, as our outward actions and the external fruits of our conscience respect men; who may moderate or restrain the external actions, wherein the outward use of our liberty consisteth; the inward liberty notwithstanding of the conscience before God, remaining entire. "[c] They greatly err," saith Calvin, "who think that their Christian liberty is nothing, unless they use it before men. But they ought to think, that by their liberty they obtain no new thing in the sight of men, but before God; and that their liberty consisteth as well in abstaining, as using. If they know, that it is a thing indifferent before God, whether they eat flesh or eggs, put on red or black apparel: it is enough and more than enough. The conscience is now loose, whereto the benefit of this liberty doth appertain; therefore, though hereafter they abstain from flesh all their life, and always wear one colour; they are nevertheless free. Yea therefore because they are free, they do with a free conscience abstain."

3. *That this also is a true liberty.* Thirdly, this liberty is spiritual, so also a true liberty. Now all true and lawful liberty of creatures, is limited and bounded; the liberty of the Creator alone, being uncircumscribed.—Wherefore if any arrogate to themselves an unbounded liberty, it is a licentiousness, and

c Instit. Lib iii. cap. 19 § 10.

not a true liberty. As first, in regard of laws and commandments of men; there are bounds set, first to the lawgivers, in respect both of the things commanded, and also of the manner of commanding. For, lawgivers may not assume unto them a liberty to command what they list, but only such things as they know not to be repugnant to the law of God. For they must know, that all their laws are limited by the law of God, and themselves upon pain of damnation, restrained from commanding that which God forbiddeth, and from forbidding that which God commandeth. For by wicked laws, they make themselves like *Jeroboam*, who caused all Israel to sin. Moreover, they must be careful, not only to command that which is lawful; but also in civil laws, those things which be expedient, and profitable for the weal public; and in laws Ecclesiastical, such things as tend [d] to decency, to order, and edification. Otherwise, though the subject may lawfully obey, in such cases; yet the lawgiver offendeth in abusing his authority, which was given him for the good of the inferiors.

Again, in respect of the manner, superiors must keep them within their bounds, and not take upon them the authority of our [e] one only lawgiver, who hath power to save, and

d 1 Cor. xiv. 26, 40, e James iv. 12.

to destroy; which is, to bind the consciences of men, as, by imposing that upon the conscience as simply necessary, which God by his law hath left indifferent; or by teaching [f] men to place religion in the observation of their traditions. For this is the practice of the Antichrist of Rome; who, usurping the authority of God, and challenging to himself a boundless power, sitteth in the consciences of men, as God.

Likewise to the subject; for as he may not think, that he hath liberty to obey any laws of men, though unlawful, and much less to place religion or perfection in the observation of them, as the Papists do; so on the other side, he may not think, that he hath liberty to break the laws of men, though not unlawful, and much less to place religion or perfection therein; as they seem to do, who use to be opposite to the Papists in the contrary extreme. For, I beseech you, do not many among us, think themselves the more religious, for refusing obedience and conformity to the laws, and censure others as formalists and time-servers? But, beloved, as we are not to judge [g] those, who out of weakness refuse conformity; so those which be refractory should not think, either the better of themselves for not conforming, or the worse of others for conforming. The kingdom [h] of God doth not stand in these things. And cer-

f Matt. xv. 2, 9. g Rom. xiv. 2, 3, &c. h Rom. xiv. 17.

tainly, if[i] neither circumcision nor uncircumcision avail any thing; then much less the use or forbearance of those ceremonies, which are in controversy among us. Doth not the Apostle plainly tell us,[k] that these outward things do not commend us unto God, and that neither the use or forbearance of them in itself doth make us either better, or worse before God? But when they be used or forborne with disobedience to lawful authority, without due regard of avoiding scandal, with uncharitable censuring and judging one of another, with alienation of the affection of one brother from another; doubtless there is fault committed. And who seeth not, that while contentions grow hot about these things, both charity and piety waxeth cold?

Secondly in respect of the creatures and things indifferent, though we have free liberty to use or forbear them, yet it is not a boundless liberty. For the law of God hath set it four bounds, viz. piety, loyalty, charity, and sobriety. *Piety*, respecting God's glory and worship; *Loyalty*, having reference to superiors; *Charity*, to all men; *Sobriety*, to ourselves. Canst thou not use thy liberty in some particular, without God's dishonour, or neglect of his service? Remember, that "whether[l] you eat or drink, or whatsoever you do, you must do all to the glory of God.

i Gal. v. 6. and vi. 15. k 1 Cor. viii. 8. l 1 Cor. x. 31.

Cannot thy liberty be used, without contempt of the Magistrate's lawful authority? Remember, that God hath commanded thee to obey thy superiors in all lawful things, as [m] all things (not forbidden by God) are lawful; that all " authority is [n] from God," and that, " he which resisteth lawful authority resisteth God;" that " they which resist, shall receive to themselves judgment;" and that thou must " obey not only for fear, but also for conscience sake." Remember what *St. Peter* saith, [o] Be subject to all human ordinance, whether the sovereign, or subordinate governors. But how? " As free, and not as having the liberty for a cloak of naughtiness, but as the servants of God." Can it not be used without the offence of thy weak brother? " Take heed," saith the Apostle, " [p] least thy liberty be an offence to the weak. For he that scandalizeth his brother, sinneth against Christ. Wherefore if meat offend my brother, I will not eat flesh while the world standeth, rather than I will offend him." Lastly, can it not be used in some particular, unless thou shalt pass the bounds of sobriety, temperance, humility, modesty, frugality, &c. Remember, what the Apostle saith, " [q] Brethren you are called to liberty, only use not your liberty, as an occasion to the flesh.

m 1 Cor. vi. 12.
n Rom. xiii. 1, 2, 5.
o 1 Peter ii. 13, 16.
p 1 Cor. viii. 9. 10, 24; Rom. xiv. 15, 16.
q Gal. v. 13.

Sect. 22. Decision of a doubtful question, what is to be done when we seem to be in a straight between disobedience to the magistrate, and offence to the weak.

But here ariseth a doubtful question, the explication whereof is needful for these times. For sometimes there seemeth to be a conflict between the law of loyalty and the law of charity; as when that which the magistrate commandeth cannot, as we think, be observed without the offence or scandal of the weak, in which case of antinomy* (which some say is our case) divers know not which way to turn them, and others erroneously choose to disobey the magistrate, rather than seem to offend their weak brethren.

Consider therefore uprightly what I shall say, and the Lord give you understanding minds and tractable hearts to see and embrace the truth.

First, therefore, understand that we are never cast into such an exigent between two sins not yet committed, but there is an issue from them both without a third. Suppose, therefore, that in this case there were an antinomy, or such an opposition between the two laws of loyalty and charity, as that the one could not be observed without the neglect of the other. In such cases of antinomy, we are to know, that if we obey the superior law, unto which we are more bound, as having higher and more

* *i. e.* Law opposed to law.—Ed.

principal ends; the inferior [a] (which giveth place unto it) is not broken. Now, the supreme end is the glory of God; then, the common salvation of the Church; then, every man's own salvation; then, the salvation of his neighbour; then, the common outward good of the Church, or Commonwealth; then, our own; then, our neighbours. So that public and common good are to be preferred before private, and spiritual before corporeal, and the glory of God before all. Well then, thou sayest thou mayest not yield to the ceremonies, as namely the surplice, the cross, and kneeling at communion; because these things cannot be done without scandalizing of thy brother. Suppose it were so, and remember that I do but suppose it. But on the other side, thou refusing the use of indifferent things, whereunto thy Christian liberty extendeth, being enjoyed by lawful authority, with such conditions as these are enjoined; I say unto thee without supposition, that besides thy disobeying the lawful authority of a Christian Church, and of a Christian Magistrate, whom thou oughtest to obey even for conscience sake; thou dost scandalize, first, thy weak brethren being affected as thyself, who by thine example, for which thou perhaps thinkest thou hast good ground, are animated,

a Matt. xii. 7; Jerem. vii. 22; Luke xiv. 26.

or, as the Apostle [b] speaketh, edified, without ground, to contemn [c] the authority of the Magistrate and of the Church; and from that contempt do many of them proceed to mislike of the State, and from mislike, either to separation, or to some degree of disloyal discontentment. Beside those of thine own disposition, thou doest offend them who are more loyally affected, who if they be not the better grounded in our [d] most holy faith, do stumble at your practice, and begin to stagger in the profession and practice of religion, when they see men seemingly most zealous in our religion, and professing (as they pretend) the cause of sincerity, upon no just cause to abandon their ministry, to oppose themselves against authority, to maintain a faction in the Church, and wilfully (for any thing that they can see) to persist in a bad cause. And hereupon many take occasion to rest in outward civility, without grace, and to mislike all forwardness in religion for your sakes, &c.

Now here seemeth to be *σκάνδαλον ἀμφίῤῥοπον*, a scandal falling two ways; indeed a single supposed offence, opposed to a double scandal, joined with disobedience. If no more could be said, who could doubt on

b 1 Cor. viii. 10.

c In this scandal they are deepest who are of greatest note.

d Judges xx.

which side rather to incline? But to these I add other respects, that ought to be regarded more than a supposed scandal. The question is not as many would seem to understand it, whether, it being a thing arbitrary and merely left unto our own choice, either to use these ceremonies, or to forbear them, (as it was in the Apostles' question of eating flesh) whether (I say) we ought to abstain, if we understood that a brother would be offended at the use of them or not: for then there were no question, but that for avoiding of scandal, we ought to abstain. But these things are not arbitrary in our choice, but imposed by lawful authority, and that with such condition, as that the observation of these things being indifferent in themselves, becometh respectively necessary. First, in respect of authority, which not only for fear, but also for conscience [e] sake, we are bound to obey in all lawful things. This one necessity of obedience is sufficient to excuse me from scandal, especially if I do my endeavour to prevent it, as after shall be shown. Secondly, in respect of the conditions wherewith they are imposed; as not to receive the communion unless we kneel; not to go on in our ministry unless we conform: for care of avoiding scandal respecteth arbitrary matters, and not necessary duties ap-

e Rom. xiii. 5.

pertaining to God's glory and our salvation; which we must perform, though all the world would be offended thereat. The care of thine own salvation must be preferred to the supposed danger of another man's fall: the care of the Church's salvation much more, the glory of God most of all. Well then, mayest thou not receive the communion, being a duty appertaining to thine own salvation, to the edification of the Church, and communion of Saints, to the glory of God, unless thou wilt receive it upon thy knees? (it being a gesture not only lawful, but most convenient to be used in such a part of God's worship, as is performed with invocation [f] on the name of God; especially seeing the gesture used at meals is not to be urged, unless the sacrament were with our meals, as at the first institution with Christ's last supper, and in the primitive Church with their love feasts, received; for the cause of the gesture being worthily taken away, the [g] reason of retaining it ceaseth; for which cause the council of Laod. c. 28, [h] as it forbade love-feasts in the Church: so also *accu-*

f I mean not only prayer, but also with thanksgiving in regard whereof it is called the Eucharist.

g So the cause of standing at the Passover ceasing, the gesture itself was altered by the Church, and that alteration confirmed by the practice of Christ (who notwithstanding perfectly fulfilled the law). Luke xxii. 14.

h Et Concil. Constantinop. in Trullo, c. 74.

bitus, the gesture used at feasts). I say unto thee confidently, if thou mayest not receive it, unless thou dost kneel, thou oughtest receive it kneeling, though another would be offended thereat.

Mayest thou not preach the word (to omit other parts of the ministerial function, the necessity whereof should prevail with us more than a supposed scandal, for it should suffice to insist in this one particular) mayest thou not, I say, preach the Gospel of Christ, being a duty whereof necessity is imposed upon thee, and [i] woe be unto thee if thou preach not the Gospel; a duty whereby thou art bound in especial manner to edify the Church, and to glorify God; unless thou yield to the use of such things, as are neither in themselves unlawful (I mean the surplice and the cross, whereof the one in the judgment of the Church serveth for decency, and the other rightly understood tendeth to edification,) neither as they are used in our Church, being neither imposed nor observed with superstition, or opinion of necessity in themselves, or of worship, as though we placed religion in them, and much less with the other popish conceits of merit, with which they observe all their traditions, or efficacy which they ascribe especially to the cross? Thou oughtest to prefer the glory of

i 1 Cor. ix. 16.

God in the salvation of his people by thy ministry, before the supposed, and perhaps but pretended, scandal of others.

Objection. Yea, but [k] we may not do evil, that good may come of it.

Answer. The question is of things indifferent. For though we may and must obey magistrates, though they be evil, yet we must obey neither good nor bad unto evil. For we must obey only in the Lord.[l]

Obj. But though the things be indifferent in themselves, yet their use may be unlawful.

Ans. That is when they be imposed either with opinion of necessity in themselves, of religion to be placed in them, of perfection or merit to be attained by them, (all which conceits our Church detesteth, as is manifest by the doctrine, whereby ceremonies are to be weighed;) or with scandal (I do not say taken,) but given to others.

Obj. Yea, but it is evil to offend my weak brother, that evil I may not do, that good may come of it.

I answer, in not yielding to conformity, thou both disobeyest the magistrate, and offendest thy weak brother too. So that when thou seemest loath to do that which is lawful and good for fear of an imagined evil; thou addest evil to evil, that is, to

k Rom. iii. 8. l Eph. v. 25.

disobedience, scandal; and besides to the most necessary duties of God's worship, preferrest the avoiding of a supposed scandal.

For all this while I speak but by supposition. For here is a supposal of antinomy or opposition of the two laws of loyalty and charity, as though one could not be observed without the breach of the other; which is not so. For where the magistrate enjoineth the use of an indifferent thing, whereat it is feared some will take offence; his duty is, for preventing the scandal, to give some time of information; that the weak may be instructed, as touching the indifferency of the thing, and the sufficiency of his authority to command it, and of their duty in submitting themselves to the observation thereof. It is also the duty of the minister to endeavour to prevent the scandal, by informing his hearers, that those things which God hath neither commanded or forbidden, are things indifferent; that no such thing is unclean in itself; that all such things are lawful; and such as whereunto Christian liberty doth extend; that in all lawful things the magistrate is to be obeyed, and therefore that these things being enjoyed, they not only may, in respect of their Christian liberty, with free conscience use them, but also must, in respect of God's commandment requiring obedience, yield to the observation of them. Which course having been taken (as it hath among us) if any will still be offended, it is peevishness and obstinacy, rather than weakness; and an offence taken, but not given: in which case, the law of charity itself doth not bind us; and that, in two respects, not yet mentioned. The one, in respect of God; the other in respect of his truth. For, I may not offend God, not to offend my brother. And it is God's truth, that Christian liberty privilegeth both Christian lawgivers (with such cautions as before have been mentioned) to ordain such laws concerning outward things, as they shall judge expedient: and also the subjects, without scrupulosity of conscience to observe them. Now, it is a principle, *Satius est nasci scandalum quam deseri verum.* "It is better a scandal should arise, than the truth to be forsaken or betrayed." Is our Christian liberty in this point called in question, whether magistrates may command such things, and whether subjects may obey? We must maintain our liberty, though others would be offended thereat. The Apostles, though for a time they yielded much to the weakness of the Jews, doing and forbearing many things, to avoid their offence, yet when their liberty [m] was called into question, they resolutely maintained it, not regarding their offence. And when, as by Peter's withdrawing himself from the Gentiles for fear of

m Gal. ii. 3, 4.

offending the Jews, the Liberty of Christians was called into question; [n] Paul withstood him to his face, and reproved him before them all, as halting in the profession of the Gospel. And so must they be content to be used, who follow Peter's example in this behalf. Thus much by the way to persuade the people to obedience and loyalty, and the ministers to conformity, which I beseech God to effect for Christ's sake.

Sect. 23. *Objections concerning Christian liberty in outward things answered.*

These things thus premised concerning the nature and quality of this peculiar liberty of Christians, it will not be hard to answer the objections of those, who run into contrary extremes concerning the same.

Object. 1. For first, on the one side, it is objected; that seeing Christ hath set us free concerning things indifferent, no man ought to restrain us; and therefore the laws commanding or forbidding the use of indifferent things, are against Christian liberty.

Whereunto I answer, first: that Christian liberty is wholly spiritual, being a liberty of the conscience and inner man, which may stand with the outward servitude of bondslaves, much more with the subjection and obedience of free subjects. For though the outward use of the liberty be moderated by

n Gal. ii. 11—14.

the Magistrate, and confined; yet the inward liberty of the conscience is not impaired, so long as the subject may obey with free conscience before God; that is, so long as the Magistrate seeketh not to bind the conscience, and to impose things not commanded of God as necessary in themselves, and as matters of religion before God, &c.

Secondly, that the liberty of Christians is a true, and therefore not an unbounded liberty. Now, one of the bounds and limits which God hath set it, is, as you have heard, the law of loyalty, requiring obedience to superiors. Wherefore a Christian man, though in respect of the inward man he be free, as being the Son of God by adoption in Christ; yet in respect of the outward man, he ought to be a servant not only to his [a] superiors, in loyalty and obedience; but also to [b] all, in benevolence and charity.

Object. 2. On the other side, it is objected, 1. That for conscience [c] sake we are to obey the Magistrate; that is, that we are bound in conscience so to do; therefore the laws and commandments of the Magistrate do bind the conscience.

Answ. It follows not, for although we are bound in conscience, to obey the lawful commandments and laws of superiors; yet that

a 1 Pet. ii. 13, 16. b Gal. v. 13. 1 Cor. ix. 19, &c. c Rom. xiii. 5.

bond is not in the particular laws of men, but in the general commandment of God.

Object. 3. Again, a thing indifferent enjoined by the Magistrate, becometh necessary [d] for Paul saith, ἀνάγκη ὑποτάσσεσθαι, it is necessary that you be subject: therefore the commandment of the Magistrate doth bind the conscience.

Answ. Neither doth this follow. For it becometh necessary, not by the particular commandment of man, but by the general commandment of God. For, notwithstanding the commandment of the Magistrate, the thing commanded remaineth indifferent in itself, and before God; and so to be used with free conscience, without placing any religion therein; howsoever it becometh necessary so far forth as by the general commandment of God, I am bound thereto. And this is that which Peter [e] saith, that we must obey Magistrates, "as free, and yet as the servants of God." Free, in respect of our consciences exempted from human power; and yet as servants of God bound in conscience to obey him in obeying them, so far forth as he doth command us to obey them.

The truth of these answers shall not only be demonstrated as it were before your eyes by a syllogism, wherein is concluded the bond of conscience, and necessity of duty in obey-

d Rom. xiii. 5. e 1 Pet. ii. 16.

ing the commandments of men, but also by other reasons proved.

The Syllogism.

All lawful commandments of Magistrates thou art bound in conscience by the law of God to obey, so far forth as he requireth such commandments to be obeyed:

This or that particular is a lawful commandment of the Magistrate:

Therefore this or that particular thou art bound in conscience by the law of God to obey, so far forth as God requireth such commandments to be obeyed.

By which argumentation we may conceive, that the distinction of necessity used in schools, viz. that there is *necessitas consequentis,* which is simple or absolute, and *necessitas consequentiæ,* which is not simple, but upon condition of other things presupposed, may not unfitly be applied to the necessity of duty imposed by the laws, either of God or man. For God's commandment imposeth the necessity as it were of the consequent, (without presupposing other things) requiring simple and absolute obedience. The law of man doth not impose the necessity of the consequent, or require simple obedience; but it imposeth only a necessity of the consequence, that is, such a necessity and no other, as may soundly be concluded from the law of God, and so far forth as it may be concluded thence. Or to speak more plainly: in a simple sentence without interpositing any condition, or presupposing any antecedent whereupon it is to be inferred, I may say, either particularly "this commandment of God is necessarily, or by necessity of duty to be obeyed," or generally, "all God's commandments are necessarily to be observed." And this speech is of necessary truth. But concerning men's commandments, if I shall say in the general, "All the commandments of men are necessarily to be observed," the speech will be false and absurd: if in particular, "this commandment of the Magistrate is necessarily to be observed:" this speech cannot be necessary simply, or by the necessity of the consequent, or (to speak more plainly for the explicating of that phrase) by the necessity of a simple sentence, wherein the consequent (or predicate) is both simply and necessarily affirmed of the antecedent or subject; it cannot, I say, be simply necessary, because (as you heard) the general is false. Notwithstanding if you presuppose these two things: first, that all lawful commandments of Magistrates are by the commandment of God necessarily to be observed, so far forth as he commandeth them to be observed: secondly, that this particular is a lawful commandment of the Magistrate; upon these premises you may prove that speech to be true by necessity of consequence, viz. that this particular commandment of the Magistrate is necessarily to be observed, &c.

But some sophister will object, that I might as well conclude thus;

Propos. All lawful commandments of the Magistrate must necessarily be obeyed:

Ass. This or that particular is a lawful commandment of the Magistrate:

Concl. Therefore necessarily to be obeyed.

I answer, that the proposition of this syllogism needeth proof, as not being manifest of itself. You will say, it may thus be proved.

Propos. What is commanded of God, must necessarily be performed.

Ass. Obedience to all lawful commandments of Magistrates is commanded of God.

Concl. Therefore obedience to all lawful commandments of Magistrates, is necessarily to be performed.

But I say again the assumption of this syllogism needeth some explanation. For the Lord would have difference put between his own commandments and the laws of men; and therefore we may not think, that he commandeth all laws of men simply to be obeyed: not simply, you must say then, but so far forth as he requireth them to be obeyed.

By which short discourse we learn, that those additions by which I explained the proposition of the syllogism, were necessary;

and that the bond of conscience is not the law of man, but of God: that we are bound to obey man's laws not simply, but so far forth as God requireth. And lastly that this speech, "All lawful commandments of Magistrates are necessarily to be obeyed," is true, not by the necessity of the consequent, as an axiom or principle which is manifest of itself; but by the necessity of consequence, as a conclusion manifested by discourse.

Now that the laws of men do not bind the conscience, it may further appear by these reasons: first, because our freedom from the laws judicial and ceremonial, which in the Scriptures is extolled for so great a benefit, would be a burthen rather than a benefit, if we should in like manner be bound to the ecclesiastical and civil laws of men. Again, if they did bind the conscience, there would be no difference between God's laws and man's laws (in respect of outward actions) and the one sort would require simple obedience as well as the other, yea unlawful commandments would also bind the conscience. But it is plain, that simple obedience is to be performed only to the laws of God. To the laws of men we are bound, not simply, but so far forth as in obeying them, we also obey God, and no further; that is, as I said, so far as God commandeth us to obey them. Now, how far forth God commandeth us to obey the laws of men, will easily appear by this distinction; for either they command such things as God forbiddeth, and forbid such things as he commandeth, (which kind of commandments are so far from binding our consciences, as that we are bound by the law of God to obey him in disobeying them:) or they command such things as God commandeth, and forbid such things as he forbiddeth, that by their authority the laws of God may the better be observed, (to which kind of commandments we are simply bound,) because as in obeying them we obey God, so in breaking them we transgress the law of God: or lastly, they command such things as God hath not forbidden, and forbid such things as God hath not commanded: to the particular commandments of this kind we are not simply bound, but so far forth as God hath commanded us to obey them; that is, as [f] free (being not simply bound to those particulars, as necessary in themselves, but using them with free conscience, as being indifferent, and therefore such, as whereunto our Christian liberty extendeth,) and yet as servants of God, thinking ourselves so far bound to observe them, "as is necessary for avoiding of scandal or contempt," which God by his law hath forbidden. Contempt: for it is necessary, saith the Apostle,[g] that we should submit ourselves to lawful authority, not only

f 1 Pet. ii. 16. g Rom. xiii. 5. 1 Pet. ii 13, 16.

for fear of punishment, but for conscience sake. For although we be free, as concerning the inner man; yet in respect of the outward man, we must as the servants of God, submit ourselves to such superiors, as God hath set over us, and not have our liberty, as a cloak of naughtiness. Scandal also is to be avoided. First, in respect of the superior, that by our disobedience we do not scan dalize or offend him. Wherein our Saviour hath given us a notable example, who, although he were (as he [h] saith) free; yet was content to pay tribute-money, for avoiding of offence. Secondly, in respect of the subject; that he stumble not at the example of our disobedience, being animated thereby to do the like. For whereas some think, that we are not to obey the Magistrate's commandment concerning a thing indifferent, if we imagine that some weak brother will be offended thereat; they greatly mistake the rule of Divines, who say these commandments are to be obeyed for avoiding scandal, and not that they are to be disobeyed for avoiding of scandal. For if this were a sufficient reason to excuse our disobedience, we should not need to obey almost any commandment of this kind, there being scarce any commandment concerning things indifferent, wherewith we may not imagine some weak and scrupu-

h Matt. xvii. 25—27.

lous conscience will be offended. But we must think ourselves more bound, for avoiding of contempt and scandal, to obey a lawful commandment, than to disobey, for avoiding a supposed offence. That which we are to do in this case, is this: If we fear any will take offence, we must labour to prevent it, by informing the party, as before hath been said. And having so done, we must do our own duty (whether he will be offended or not) in obeying the lawful commandment of the Magistrate, so far as it shall be necessary for avoiding of scandal and contempt.

Sect. 24. The liberty of Glory. Hitherto I have intreated of the liberty of grace, both that which is common to the faithful in all ages; and also that which is peculiar to Christians under the Gospel. There remaineth (in a word to be spoken of) the liberty of glory; which is not only a perfect deliverance from sin, misery, and all imperfections, (whereunto because we are subject [a] in this life, for here is as, *Augustine* saith, *inchoata, non perfecta libertas,* we ought to aspire towards this perfection) but also a fruition of happiness and all the privileges of the citizens of heaven.

This liberty is either of the soul alone, as at our death; when we may freely and with

a Rom. vii. 24.

comfort resign our souls into the hands of God, that he may commit the same to the [b] blessed Angels to be transported into heaven, where we are unto the end of the world, comfortably to expect our full redemption. Or it is of the body also at the day of judgment (and is therefore called [c] the redemption of our body) when it rising unto glory, shall be freed from the servitude [d] of corruption, this [e] mortal putting on immortality, and this corruptible putting on incorruption; that death being swallowed up in victory, we may enjoy, both in our bodies and souls, the [f] glorious liberty of God's children in the kingdom of heaven. This ought we with earnestness of desire [g] to aspire unto, and with certainty of [h] faith to expect; that thereby we may be weaned from the world, having [i] our conversation in heaven; and not either by the desires of the world (which are but [k] vanities) be allured and ensnared, or by the terrors thereof, (which are not [l] worthy the glory that shall be revealed,) drawn into bondage.

Thus have you heard the doctrine of Christian liberty. Now hear the use.

b Luke xvi. 22.
c. Rom. viii. 23.
d Rom. viii. 11.
e 1 Cor. xv. 53, 54.
f Rom. viii. 21.
g Rom. viii. 22, 23.
h Titus ii. 13.; Luke xxi. 28.
i Phil. iii. 20.
k Eccles. i. 2.
l Rom. viii. 18.

Sect. 25. The application or use.

For seeing this liberty is a benefit of so great excellency in itself, and of such profit and necessity to us: Our first duty is, to try and examine ourselves by that which hath been said, whether we have as yet obtained this liberty or not. If not, (as [a] "he which committeth sin, is the servant of sin") we must labour to acknowledge and feel that miserable servitude, wherein we are, under sin and Satan (for he that is not free, and yet feeleth not his bondage, is drowned in sin, even as he that is over head and ears in the water, feeleth no weight thereof) that in the sense of our misery we may not only truly and earnestly desire; but also carefully use all means to attain this liberty, and never be at rest, until we have obtained it. It is strange to see what hard services men will undergo, and what great sums they will forego, to get an earthly freedom, while this spiritual freedom, which is worth many worlds, will scarcely be accepted, when men are called and invited unto it. Which sheweth, that men naturally, are not only servants, but willingly and wilfully continue in servitude. But you will say, what means are we to use? I answer, 1. Diligently and conscionably to hear the Word, as being the

a John viii. 34.

means, which God hath ordained to call you to liberty. 2. To ask, seek, knock by earnest and hearty prayer, unto God the author of this liberty, that he would give you the spirit of liberty. 3. To turn unto God unfeignedly, laying hold upon Christ by faith, and repenting of your sins. *Eris liber,* saith *Augustine,*[b] *si fueris servus, liber peccati, servas justitiæ :* You shall be free from sin, if you will become the servants of righteousness. If God hath already called us unto this liberty, our duty is two-fold, both which the Aposle mentioned, Gal. v. 1. the one,[c] that "we stand fast in this liberty, wherewith Christ Jesus hath made us free, and not suffer ourselves to be entangled again with the yoke of bondage." And the rather we must be careful to stand fast in this liberty, because it is mightily assaulted by all the enemies of our salvation, the flesh, the world, the devil. Now, we are to stand steadfast, both in the doctrine of Christian liberty, which is the doctrine of the Gospel, and not suffer ourselves to be allured, or intoxicated, either with the golden[d] cup of the Babylonian strumpet, the Church of Rome, which doth not only bereave men of Christian liberty, but also draw them into Antichristian bondage: or with the Cyrcean cup of the Liber-

b August. in John. tract. 41. c Gal. v. 1.
d Apoc. xvii. 4, xviii. 3.

tines, which transformeth Christianism into Epicurism, and the liberty of the spirit into the liberty of the flesh. And we are also to be steadfast and resolute in the practice of Christian liberty: as of vocation, not to be entangled again with the servitude of sin and Satan, (for if having professed ourselves freed thereof, we be again entangled therein, our latter end, as *St. Peter* saith,[e] will be worse than our beginning.) Of justification, as not to subject ourselves to the law's exaction of inherent and perfect righteousness to justification, (for they which are [f] of the works of the law, are under the curse) but without regard of our own righteousness, to rely wholly for our justification on the mercies of God, and merits of Christ apprehended by faith; and to hold him [g] accursed, though he were an angel from heaven, that should teach otherwise. Of sanctification, as not to subject ourselves to the dominion [h] of sin, or to the terror or rigour of the law; but without servile fear, willingly and cheerfully to serve our heavenly Father, being well assured that he will cover our wants, and accept of our unperfect endeavours. Of Christian liberty in respect of outward things; as not to suffer our consciences to be bound by the authority of any creature, enjoying them as necessary

e 2 Peter ii. 20, 21.
f Gal. iii. 10.
g Gal. i. 8.
h Rom. vi. 12.

in themselves, and much less to bind our own consciences, as scrupulously and superstitiously putting religion either in the use or forbearance of them. Of the glorious liberty, as not to suffer ourselves by all the machinations of the world, the flesh and the devil, to be withdrawn from the hope and expectation of it; but comfortably to live as men [i] saved in hope.

The other duty, is that which the Apostle mentioneth, Gala. v. 13. "Brethren," saith he, [k] "you are called to liberty; only use not your liberty as an occasion to the flesh, but by charity serve one another." This is, that

The abuse of Christian liberty.

we should be careful, both to avoid the abuse of Christian liberty, and also to use it aright. The abuse is manifold. As first, of the saving grace of God; when men do turn [l] it into wantonness, their freedom from sin, into a freedom to sin as though they were so freed from the law; as that they need not to obey it; as though good works, because they are not exacted to justification, were in no respect needful to salvation. "We are not free," saith *Luther*,[m] "by faith in Christ from works, but from the opinion of works, that is, from the foolish presumption of justification sought by works." Secondly, of Christian liberty,

i Rom. viii. 24.
k Gal. v. 13.
l Jude iv.
m De libert. Christ.

in respect of the creatures of God, and the use of things indifferent; when we do use them without regard of our duty, to God, our neighbour, or ourselves.

The duty which we owe to God, is piety; to our neighbour in general, charity; and in particular to our superior, obedience and loyalty; to ourselves, sobriety. For these, as I said, are the bounds of our liberty, which if we pass in the use thereof, we abuse it. The use of our liberty is contrary to piety: First, when we ourselves are impious, and irreligious. For though the things in themselves be clean, yet the use of them is unclean to them that are impure. For as [n] to the pure, all things are pure, so to the unclean nothing is clean. Secondly, when the use of them is not sanctified unto us,[o] either by the Word, as when we make more indifferent things, than God in his word hath made, as drunkenness, fornication, usury, &c. or when we do not use them in faith and sound persuasion out of the word of God, which is the charter of our liberty, that we may lawfully and with a good conscience use them (for though nothing in itself be unclean, yet to him [p] that thinketh or doubteth that it is unclean, it is so to him; for as the Apostle, speaking of this particular, saith, "Whatsoever is not

n Titus i. 5. o Tim. iv. 15.
p Rom. xiv. 14, 23.

faith, is sin :) or by the duties of invocation, as the use of meat and drink, without either prayer to God for his blessing in the use, or thanksgiving for the same. Thirdly, we abuse our liberty irreligiously, when we use it to the dishonour of God, or to the hindrance of his worship and service, as in the immoderate and unseasonable use of recreations, &c. whereby men shew themselves to be [q] lovers of pleasure more than of God.

Likewise our use of the creatures, and of things indifferent, is against charity, when we use them without due regard of avoiding scandal and offence. Against loyalty, when using our liberty with contempt of lawful authority, we make it a cloak to cover some naughtiness. And lastly, against sobriety, when under the pretence of Christian liberty, the creatures of God, and other things indifferent, are used, either as instruments to serve, or as ensigns to display, our pride or intemperate lusts, as in the excess of meat and drink, recreations, the use of the marriage bed, apparel, buildings, and such like.

Sect. 26. The right use of Christian liberty. But let us come to the right use of our Christian liberty; which is two-fold, either the sanctification of our lives, or the pacification of our consciences. As touching the

q φιλήδονει μᾶλλον ἢ φιλόθεοι; 2 Tim. iii. 4.

former: the right use of the liberty of saving grace is, when it is used to the free, voluntary, and cheerful worship and service of God, in holiness and righteousness, for [a] that is the end of our liberty and redemption. The right use of Christian liberty in outward things, is, when it is used to a free and cheerful serving, both one of [b] another in charity, and of the superior in obedience and loyalty; that being free [c] from all, we make ourselves servants unto all, for their good. For as *Luther* saith, "[d] A Christian in respect of the inner man, is free, but in respect of the outward man he is (through charity) the servant of all." And herein we are to imitate the example of Christ; who, [e] though he were God, took upon him the form of a servant to make us free; and though he were the Lord of all, [f] came not to be ministered unto, but to minister. And likewise of the blessed angels; who, though they be glorious spirits, notwithstanding take no scorn to be sent forth into the [g] ministry and service of our good.

The right use of the doctrine concerning the liberty of glory, is, truly to believe it, and to live as in expectation of it; knowing, that he which hath this [h] hope, that he shall be like unto Christ at his appearance, will

a Luke i. 74, 75.
b Gal. v. 13.
c 1 Cor. ix. 19.
d De libert. Christ.
e Philp. ii. 5, 6.
f Matt. xx. 28.
g Heb. i. 14
h 1 John iii. 3.

purify himself, as he is pure; that as he hopes to be like him, in respect of the liberty of glory, so he may in some measure resemble his graciousness, by the liberty of grace.

But the chief use of this doctrine, is, to pacify men's consciences; without which (unless they sleep in carnal security) they are so wonderfully perplexed, that neither can they live in peace nor attempt any thing almost with quiet minds. For whereas there be four things which trouble perplexed consciences, this doctrine is a sovereign remedy to clear and to appease the conscience, in respect of them all. The first, is the guilt of sin, and fear of damnation. For when thy conscience is summoned before the judgment seat of God, or terrified with the apprehension of his wrath, as in time of temptation, or affliction, or in the hour of death; when thou dost consider the severity of God's justice, who will not suffer sin to go unpunished, the rigour of the law, denouncing the curse of God against every even the least transgression, the testimony of thine own conscience, which is instead of a thousand witnesses, accusing and condemning thee of innumerable transgressions; how canst thou think of appearing before God, who is greater than thy conscience, to be justified or condemned, without horror of conscience, and confusion of mind? But blessed be God, who hath granted us this liberty of grace, that in the question of justification, whereby in this life we are freed from fear of damnation, and entitled unto the kingdom of heaven, we need not look into our obedience, or to the sentence of the law ; but may be assured, if we believe in Christ, that God doth justify us, being sinners in ourselves, without respect of our works; that he hath freed us from the law's exaction of inherent righteousness, to the acceptation of our persons; that he imputing the righteousness of Christ to the believer, accepteth of him as righteous in Christ; that the faithful man hath liberty to appeal from the tribunal of justice, to the throne of grace, from the sentence of the law, to the promise of the Gospel, and renouncing his own righteousness, yea esteeming it as dung in the question of justification, to rest alone in the mercies of God, and merits of Christ.

But because the world is so apt to abuse this most comfortable doctrine, and to turn gracious liberty into carnal licentiousness ; it shall be needful to add this caution : That howsoever we are by our justification in this life entitled unto the kingdom of heaven ; and although by the righteousness and merits of Christ alone apprehended by faith, we are both justified and also saved : yet for as much as many deceive themselves with an idle conceit of faith, and with a vain presumption that they are justified, when notwithstanding [i]

i Prov. xxx. 12.

they remain in their sins; therefore we must think it most necessary, being once justified by faith, and entitled unto the kingdom of heaven, to demonstrate our faith, and our justification by a godly life; walking in that way of good works, which God hath[k] prepared for us to walk in towards our country in heaven. For though we are justified and saved by the merits of Christ alone apprehended by faith; notwithstanding sanctification is the[l] cognizance of them that are saved, and good works are the evidence, according[m] unto which God will pronounce the sentence of salvation. For as the tree[n] is known by his fruit; so he that[o] worketh righteousness, is righteous, and in like manner by sanctification our justification is manifested. For true faith[p] worketh by love, and good works are as the breathing of a lively faith. And therefore though faith alone doth justify, as Paul[q] teacheth, because it alone doth apprehend the righteousness of Christ unto justification; yet as St. James[r] teacheth, that faith which alone severed from obedience doth not justify, neither alone, nor at all, because it is not a true faith. For even as the body without breathing is known to be dead;[s] so faith

k Eph. ii. 10. l Acts xx. 32. m Rom. ii. 6.
n Luke vi. 44. o 1 John iii. 7. p Gal. v. 6.
q Gal. ii. 16. Rom. iii. 28. r James ii. 14, &c.
s James ii. 16.

without works is dead. We are therefore justified in this life, and entitled unto the kingdom of heaven, as to our inheritance, by faith without [t] works; but none are actually saved, nor inherit that kingdom in the life to come, but such as first are sanctified. For as our Saviour saith, we have indeed not only remission of sins by faith, but also by faith we have our inheritance; but yet, as he saith, [u] among them that are sanctified.

The second is the conscience of our manifold wants and imperfections, in those duties which we do perform. For how can a man be persuaded that God, to [x] whom no creature being compared is pure, will allow of his imperfect and stained obedience. And if he be not persuaded, that his service is acceptable unto God, with what heart can he perform it. The doctrine therefore of Christian liberty assureth our consciences, that we are freed from the law's exaction of perfect obedience, to the acceptation of our actions: that God covering our imperfections, as an indulgent Father, with the perfect righteousness and obedience of Christ, imputeth not our wants unto us, but accepteth of the truth of our will and desire for the deed, and our sincere endeavour for the perfect perform-

t Rom. iv. 6. u Acts xxvi. 18.
x John xv. 14. xvi. 16.

ance. And therefore a Christian may, in respect of this liberty, with comfort and cheerfulness perform obedience, according to the measure of grace received, being assured that our defective and stained obedience, will be accepted of God through the mediation and intercession of Jesus Christ.

The third is the scruple of conscience, concerning the use of outward things, how far forth they may be used or forborne. For if a man be not rightly informed herein, there will be no end[y] of scrupulosity and superstition. From this scruple also, the doctrine of Christian liberty doth free us: assuring us, that to all these things our liberty doth extend, either to use them freely, or freely to forbear them; and that nothing is unclean in itself, nor yet unto us, if we be so persuaded; and that to the clean, all things are clean, provided always, that the use of this liberty be kept within the bounds before-mentioned, of piety, charity, loyalty, and sobriety.

The fourth and last is the horror of conscience in the hour of death. For can a man with comfort give up his soul to be severed from the body, when he knoweth not, either what will become of his soul after the separation thereof from the body, or how, and in what case his body shall rise again. But this

y Vide Calv. Inst. lib. 3. cap. xix. 7.

doctrine doth assure us, that Christ hath purchased, not only a liberty of grace in this life, but also of glory for our souls against the end of our life, and for our bodies also, against the day of judgment. So that we[z] have liberty or boldness, to enter into the holy places by the blood of Jesus, by the new and living way, which he hath prepared for us through the vail, that is to say, his flesh; being assured, that by reason of our union with Christ, we are risen [a] again with Christ, and with him set in the heavenly places, whither he is ascended[b] to prepare a place for us: and from whence he will come again to bring us thither, that where he is, there we may be also. Wherefore in respect of this liberty, the faithful may with comfort, both surrender our souls into the hands of God our merciful Father, and also bequeath our bodies to the earth, in full assurance that our souls shall by the Angels be translated into heaven, and that our bodies shall at the day of judgment, be freed from the servitude of corruption, and rise again to glory: this mortal having put on immortality, and this corruptible incorruption, that it being again reunited to the soul, we may for ever and ever, enjoy both in body and soul, the glo-

z Heb. x. 19, 20. a Eph. ii. 6.
b John xiv. 2, 3, and xvii. 24. Philip iii. 20, 21.

rious liberty of the citizens of heaven. Unto which liberty of glory may he bring us, who hath so dearly purchased it for us, even Christ Jesus the righteous; to whom with the Father and the holy Ghost, be eternal praise and glory. Amen.

FINIS.

J. Dennett, Printer, Leather Lane.